ART NOUVEAU JEWELLERY & FANS

gabriel mourey, aymer vallance, et al.

DOVER PUBLICATIONS, INC., NEW YORK

Published in Canada by General Publishing Company, Ltd., 30 Lesmill Road, Don Mills, Toronto, Ontario.
Published in the United Kingdom by Constable and Company, Ltd., 10 Orange Street, London WC 2.

This Dover edition, first published in 1973, is a republication of the complete text and all but one of the plates from the work originally titled *Modern Design in Jewellery and Fans: by the Artist Craftsmen of Paris, London, Vienna, Berlin, Brussels, Etc.* [no date]. [The plate omitted was not in the Art Nouveau style.] The pages and plates have been renumbered and a new Table of Contents and Index of Designers have been added. Several of the plates which were originally printed in color are here shown in black and white.

International Standard Book Number: 0-486-22961-0
Library of Congress Catalog Card Number: 73-75871

Manufactured in the United States of America
Dover Publications, Inc.
180 Varick Street
New York, N.Y. 10014

Contents and Illustrations

BRITISH JEWELLERY AND FANS, BY AYMER VALLANCE 41

AUSTRIAN JEWELLERY, BY W. FRED 97

MODERN FRENCH JEWELLERY & FANS. BY GABRIEL MOUREY.

FRENCH superiority in the art of jewellery seems to be incontestable to-day. No unbiassed observer will deny the fact that with us there is more richness, more variety, more originality than can be found elsewhere; and the jewellery section in the Esplanade des Invalides at the Exhibition of 1900 showed to the whole world the progress made in this special branch of applied art by our craftsmen and our artists; showed, too, the *verve*, the imagination, the fancifulness, which are the special property of the French race in all that relates to articles of luxury, to those things which are essentially "useless," if so we may term a woman's adornments; if so we may regard the beauty of precious stones, of enamels skilfully and subtly formed—of all that, in a word, which, taken from Nature's infinite treasure-house, serves to constitute that adorably vain, that exquisitely superfluous thing—the jewel. Ruskin once remarked, in his strange, penetrating way, that the loveliest things are those which are the least useful—lilies and peacocks' feathers, for instance. Furthermore, to depreciate the part played by jewellery in relation to decorative art would be equivalent to minimising the *rôle* of womankind in civilisation. Then, again, as regards decoration or adornment, has not the highest mission devolved on woman? Has she not had to assume the most active part in it all? The modern jewellery vogue has, I am convinced, done more in France to propagate new ideas in the way of decorative art than all the æsthetic theories ever evolved, however sound.

ONE might say much, might make many reflections on this renascence of the jeweller's art, as manifested at the present moment in Paris. This revival reveals itself rich and abundant—perhaps too rich and abundant; but what of the future? What fruit will it bear when the glamour of that which it has already borne has passed away? Is there no danger of seeing good intentions miscarry —high gifts falling into excesses injurious to the prosperity of the movement? Is not the new fashion—if it be merely a fashion— being adopted with too much enthusiasm, followed with too much ardour, to last ? Is there no fear of a reaction ? Here are several questions to which we cannot reply with any certainty.

YET, what matter ? Among the works produced during the past five years or so—that is, since the full expansion of the movement—there are many which, by their originality, their technical perfection, deserve to remain. And remain they certainly will, to bear witness to the audacious fancy, the creative faculty of our artists, and as a sort of passionate homage laid by the men of to-day at the feet of the Eternal Feminine.

* * *

THE name of M. René Lalique arises instinctively as soon as one begins to discuss the modern jewel. He is the renovator, or, preferably, the creator, of the art as we know it nowadays, and one can easily understand the enthusiasm and the admiration aroused by his work. M. Lalique is almost as celebrated as M. Edmond Rostand ; and he at least deserves his celebrity, for he is a real, a very great, artist. And such he must indeed be to be able to make one forget his imitators, many of whose productions are as detestable as copies can be. At times even—most unjustly, I admit—one almost comes to hate the art of M. Lalique himself, so persistently is it badly imitated. One has been constrained before now to hate Raphael, on seeing a Cabanel or a Bouguereau ! But enough of that !

THE jewels by M. Lalique now reproduced are rather different, both in conception and in treatment, from his usual manner. Here he appears as a more direct observer of Nature, more devoted to simplicity and breadth. His new combs, with pansy- and sycamore-leaf *motifs*, in horn and silver—especially the exquisite one with sycamore seeds in horn, silex, black enamel, and obsidian, with golden insects here and there—show him still anxious to extend the field of his experiments, never tired of seeking fresh subjects and testing new materials. Instead of remaining stationary and falling asleep at his post, he is spurred by a desire for conquest, and shows himself ever fertile in imagination, of infinite fancy, constantly advancing, with undiminished freedom and originality.

AT the Universal Exhibition the works executed by M. Vever, in collaboration with M. Eugène Grasset, obtained the success that was their due. But the most important piece of work achieved by these two artists was not finished at that time. I refer to the sumptuous and heroic pendant of Hercules, which we are fortunate enough to be able to reproduce here from the original water-colour by M. Grasset. It is truly an admirable work, one in which all the imaginative and technical qualities possessed by the illustrator of the " Quatre Fils Aymon" are to be seen in profusion. What richness, what distinction in the details; what perfection of balance, both in design and in colouring ! As for the execution by the firm of Vever, they deserve as much credit for it as if they had produced an original work. This is a jewel worthy to find a permanent place in one of the great European galleries, to rank side by side with the wonderful productions of the past.

M. GEORGES FOUQUET is a most daring *fantaisiste*, and his creations impress one by qualities altogether different from those of the MM. Vever. He might perhaps be said to belong to the Lalique school, not that he imitates him, but by reason of his imaginative gifts. He is generally complicated, somewhat Byzantine, and thoroughly modern in any case. Some of his jewels would, I think, gain by being less rich ; nevertheless, they are very interesting, and they deserve all the success they have won. The chief objection that can be urged against them is their lack of spontaneity. M. Georges Fouquet certainly holds a foremost place in the new movement. Already his production is considerable. Altogether an artist of rare gifts and splendid audacity.

I HAVE always had a liking for the jewellery of M. Colonna—for some of it, at any rate, that which is most simple, most original, and most wearable. His works have this great charm in my eyes, that they are neither show-case jewels nor mere *bijoux de parade*, things intended solely for display. As a rule, they are quiet and practical. In most cases they have no " subject," being simply happy combinations of lines and curves and reliefs, the *imprévu* of which has a particular charm.

M. MARCEL BING, all of whose productions, like those of M. Colonna, are the monopoly of the " Art Nouveau Bing," has done some delightful things. One can see that he is still somewhat timid and hesitating, but his taste is sure, and he has an imagination which, if not specially abundant, is at least delicate and fine. He has a sense of colour too, and his pretty fancies are carried out with evident delight.

"LA MAISON MODERNE," so actively directed by M. Meier-Graefe, has produced a large number of jewels. Ordinarily the designs are supplied by MM. Maurice Dufrène, Paul Follot, and Orazzi. Of course, they are not of uniform merit, but this in no way diminishes the interest attaching to their efforts. They are marred to some extent, it must be admitted, by certain extravagances, but even that is better than a relapse into the old *formulæ*, or the profitless reproduction of the bad models which were the rage some thirty years since. Moreover, " La Maison Moderne "—all praise to it !—has brought within the reach of the public quantities of jewellery which, without being masterpieces of conception or execution, are yet thoroughly good work based on excellent principles of novelty and freshness. They are what may be termed " popular " jewels.

THE works designed by M. Théodore Lambert, and executed by M. Paul Templier, are of altogether different character. In these days, when excessive complications in jewel-work are so general and so much esteemed, these rings, necklaces and *plaques*, with their symmetrical linear designs in monochrome or reddish or greenish metal, relieved at times by pearls only, and with their formal *ajourements*, will doubtless seem to many people too simple or too commonplace. It will be justly urged against them that they are not sufficiently symbolic, that they take no account of the human form. No nymph disports herself amid the fall of the leaves in a lake of enamel bordered by water-lilies and iris blooms ; no serpent no devil-fish winds about in spasmodic contortions : yet these are charming works of art, beautifully and harmoniously designed, and with lines balanced to perfection. They are, in fact, jewels meant to be worn, *bijoux de ville*, which, while attracting no special notice, form nevertheless most exquisite objects of female adornment.

M. RENÉ FOY is a strange artist, rather restless, never altogether satisfied with himself, and haunted by a perpetual desire for something novel. Is he completely himself, that which he wishes or strives to be ? This is the question those who have closely watched his career are asking themselves. For my part, I know some delightful things of his, extraordinarily delicate and graceful ; but I also remember some of his work in which his exaggerations are such that one despairs of understanding his meaning. Unless I greatly mistake him, he wants the jewel to express more than it is possible for the jewel to express, and therefore is continually restless in his attempts to achieve the unachievable. He loses himself in a maze of " refinements " which, in my opinion, are outside the limits of the art he practises. He has created lovely things, things so novel as to be almost too novel, but I do not think he has said his final word yet. He is a young man who may have many surprises in store for us.

THE jewels of M. Jules Desbois are works of pure sculpture. His vision, at once broad and delicate, takes the form of beautiful female forms in dreamy or voluptuous attitude, sleeping amid the masses of their abundant hair, against a background of gold, or shell, or whatever the material may be. Any womanly gesture suffices ; and, in truth, what more is needed to make a real work of art in the form of a brooch or a button ? No conventional flowers, no complicated interlacements, nothing "decorative" in the bad sense of the word ; yet his work is powerfully and delicately modern. M. Desbois' jewels are perfect pieces of sculpture.

VICTOR PROUVÉ, the painter, has been influenced in a similar way, but, not being a regular sculptor, he is more complicated without being any more original on that account. There is more "composition" in his jewels than in those of M. Desbois, more real, more visible, intention. His waistbelts, his brooches, &c., are admirably suited to the purpose for which they are intended, their modelling being full, supple, and keen. The jewels, executed with scrupulous care and irreproachable *technique* by M. Rivaud, are real works of art.

M. BECKER and M. Paul Richard, who are both working almost exclusively for M. Ferdinand Verger ("F. V." is the trademark of the firm), incline to that type of jewellery which might be termed "sculptured." They are very conscientious artists, but in my opinion, at any rate, the originality there may be within them has not yet made itself fully apparent.

M. LOUIS BONNY'S jewels deserve special attention. Like M. Vever, M. Bonny shows a predilection for precious stones, which he has the art of using with rare originality. At the last *salon* of the Société des Artistes Français he exhibited a series of jewels which attracted much attention, among them—in addition to a beautiful necklace of wild grape in enamel, diamonds, and emerald, in addition to various floral pendants and neck ornaments in enamel and diamonds—a curious diadem, representing cocks in gold and enamel fighting for possession of a superb topaz. This was a real *tour de force* in the way of execution. Other beautiful things of his I know, particularly his *plaque de cou* of geraniums, with the leaves in diamonds, the flowers in rubies, the stems and buds in dark green enamel, the whole being at once rich and sober in colouring and most harmoniously and flexibly composed.

M. JOÉ DESCOMPS is a sound artist, whose efforts, laudable as they may be, nevertheless lack boldness. He has imagination enough, but it looks as though he feared to give it rein. With a little less timidity M. Descomps would doubtless produce something more piquant and more fresh.

I GREATLY like the work of M. Charles Rivaud. It displays a love of simplicity too often wanting in the productions of many of his fellow artists. If his jewels recall—without imitating—the ornamental jewellery of Egypt or Greece, those of primitive civilisations or those sorts popular in Russia, I can see no harm in the fact. Better for him and for us that he should turn to these inexhaustible springs than become a mere imitator of other imitators of successful jewellers. His rings and his necklaces, in which he is always careful to leave to the materials employed all the natural charm they possess, are productions which will please the artist rather than the *bourgeois* and the " snob." They are discreet and honest, never loud or eccentric.

NO less interesting, in another way, are the jewels by M. Mangeant and M. Jacquin. It is urged against them that they are crude, incomplete and imperfect in execution. The truth is, these two artists—whom I bring into conjunction, although their work is dissimilar, save from their common regard for freedom in the use of materials—have, above all, a love for natural forms. Out of a flower, a piece of seaweed, or any humble *motif*, vegetable or animal, they construct jewels in gold or oxidised silver, discreetly relieved by stones, which, if of no great intrinsic value, are nevertheless highly decorative. M. Mangeant, with mother-of-pearl and hammered *repoussé* silver, has created charming jewels, in which all the constructive parts have been intentionally left visible. Professional jewellers shrug their shoulders at the sight of these jewels, which bear so plainly the stamp of the hand that fashioned them. Yet, in their *naïve* rudeness, they appeal to me far more forcibly than does the polychromatic tin-ware of so many highly-esteemed producers.

M. CHARLES BOUTET DE MONVEL, although gifted with a richer and subtler imagination, may be included in this little group. In certain of his jewels there is, as it were, a reminiscence of Byzantine art—in this owl-comb, for instance, which I regard as one of his best works. His swan hairpin, his seaweed buttons in gold and silver on greenish enamel with a pearl in the centre, his *plaque de cou* in translucid enamel, are also strong and captivating. His sunshade handles too, and his scarf-pins, are full of delicate fancy.

IT is impossible, within the space at my disposal, to describe in detail the productions of many other workers well worthy of extended mention. Let it suffice, therefore, to cite the names of M. Henri Nocq, that fresh and bold artist; of M. and Mme.

Pierre Selmersheim ; M. Feuillâtre ; Mme. Annie Noufflard ; MM. Haas, Cherrier, Chalon, Falguières, Dabault, G. Laffitte, Houillon, Archambault, L. H. Ruffe, Quénard, Blanchot, Muret, Desrosiers, Le Couteux, Marioton, Lucien Hirtz, and Nau—artists who work, some on their own account, some for the big jewellery firms.

OF the firms in question one must in justice name in the first place those of Boucheron and Falize frères, not forgetting L. Aucoc, Vever, Sandoz, Lucien Gaillard, Fouquet, Desprès, Teterger, Chaumet, Templier, Ferdinand Verger, J. Duval, Coulon, and Piel frères.

SUCH, briefly, is the modern art-jewellery movement in France. Its intensity, as one sees, is so great as to be almost alarming. Whither is it tending ? Some of its excesses are dangerous ; what will be the result ? M. Emile Molinier, in a recent article on " Objects of Art in the Salons of 1901," expresses certain fears which I share. He dreads a reaction due to the eccentricities of certain artists, to their love of the outrageous and the *bizarre*, to their lack of proportion, both in form and in choice of material.

" IT would really be a pity," he says, " if so promising a revival of the true artistic jewellery should come to a bad end. Happily we have not reached that point yet, but it is a result which may soon be reached if artists continue to foist these weird things on the public. A fashion in jewellery should last longer than a fashion in dresses or in hats ; but it should not be forgotten that it must rely in the long run on its appropriateness and adaptability." My sincere hope is that these fears may prove to be groundless.

GABRIEL MOUREY.

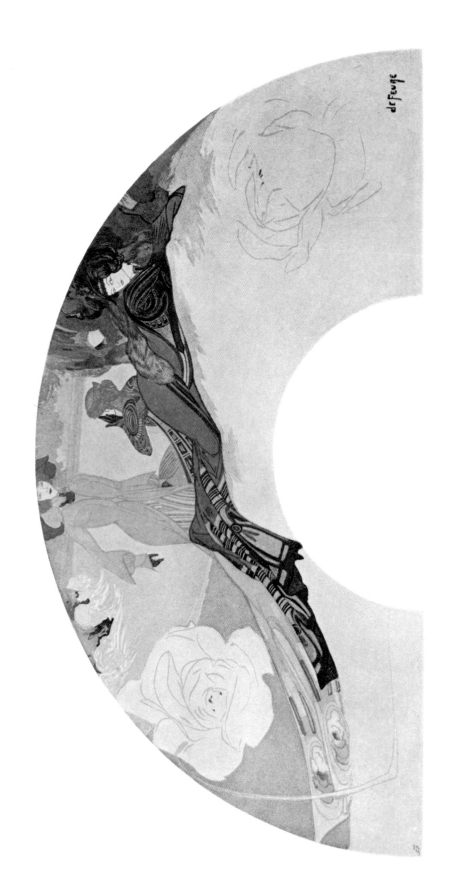

Design for a Fan
GEORGES DE FEURE

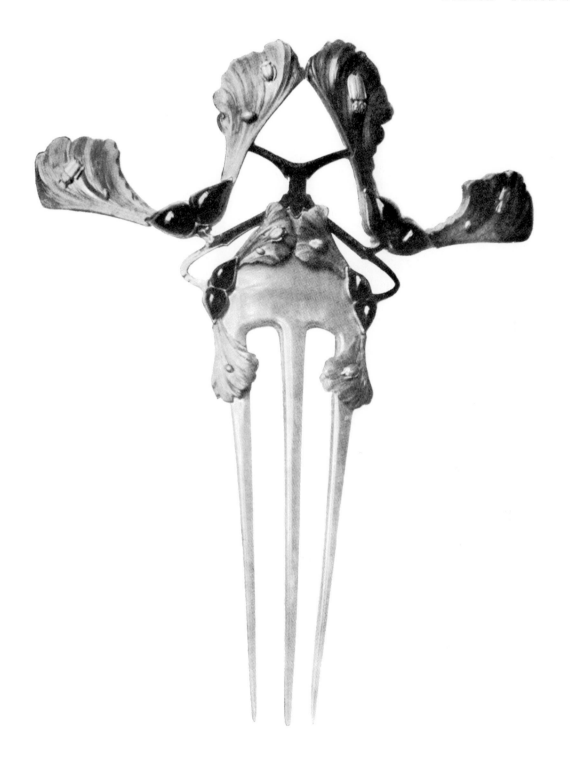

Comb in Horn, Silex, Black Enamel and Obsidian.   Insects in Gold

RENÉ LALIQUE

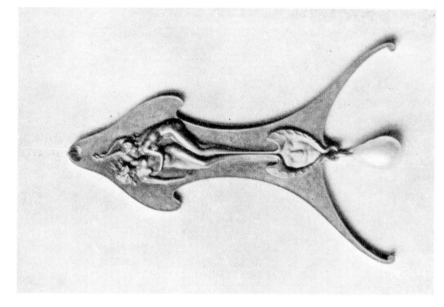

FIG. B

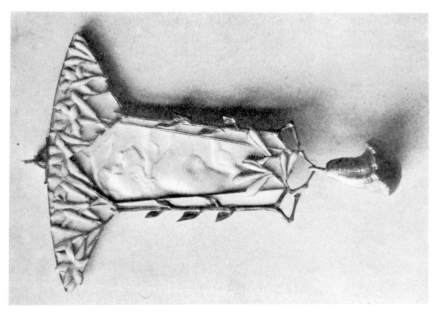

FIG. A

A. *Pendant in Gold, Ivory, Enamel and Pearl*
B. *Pendant in Gold, Enamel and Pearl*
      RENÉ LALIQUE

Watch in Ivory, Gold and Enamel
Clasp, Leaves of Plane Tree, in Silver

RENÉ LALIQUE

PLATE 5   FRENCH

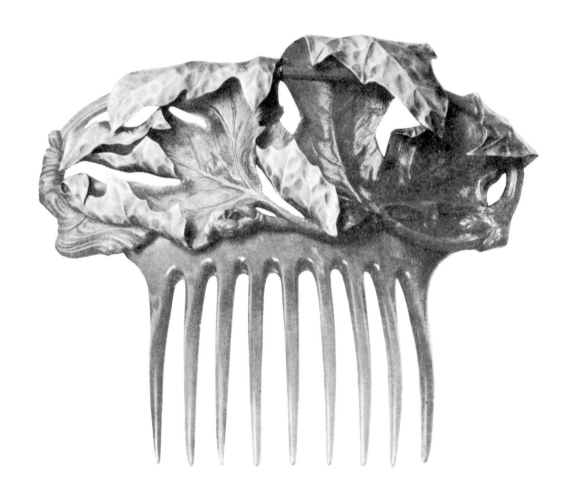

Comb, Leaves of Sycamore
Horn and Silver

RENÉ LALIQUE

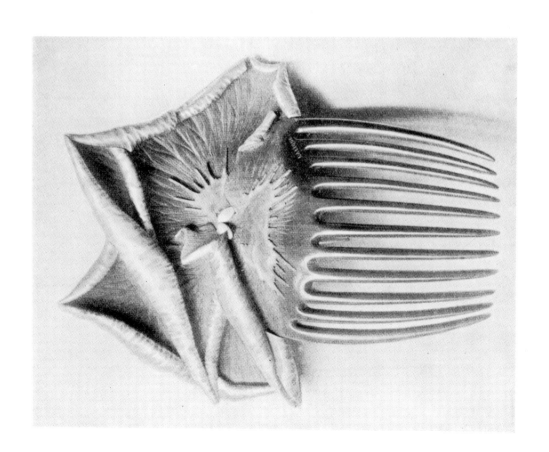

Combs in Horn and Silver
RENÉ LALIQUE

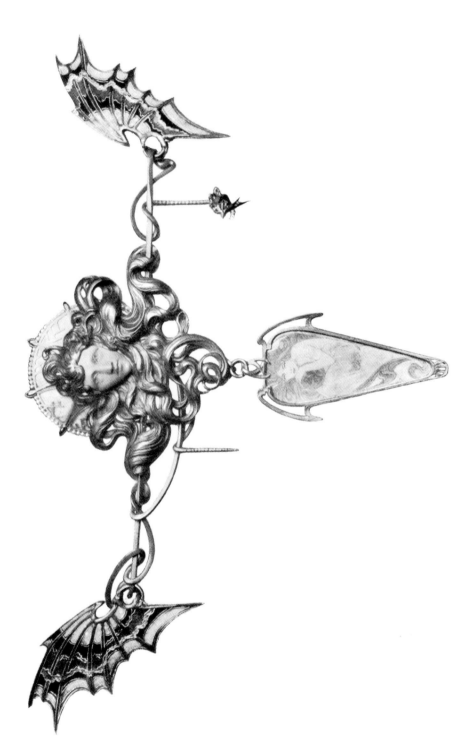

Parure de Corsage, in Gold and Enamels
MUCHA and G. FOUQUET

Girdle with Pendants in Gold,
Pearls and Brilliants
G. FOUQUET

PLATE 9   FRENCH

Necklet with Pendant,
Gold and Enamel
G. FOUQUET

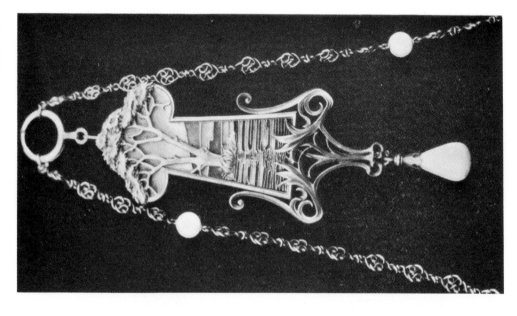

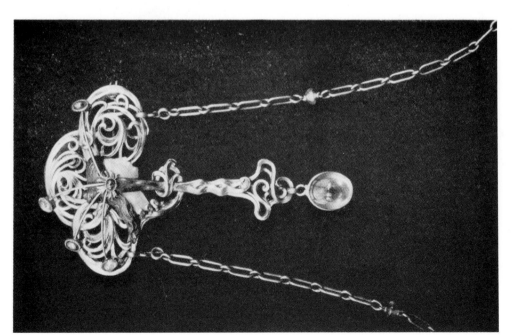

FIG. B

FIG. A

A. Pendant in Gold, Enamel and Stones
B. Pendant in Gold, Enamel and Pearls

G. FOUQUET

PLATE 11   FRENCH

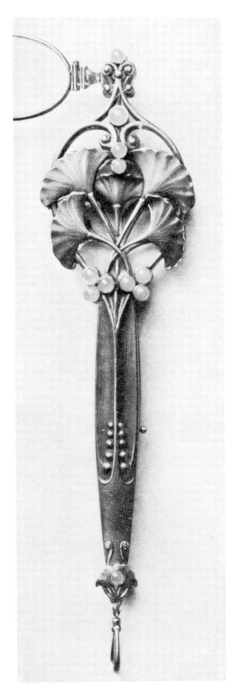

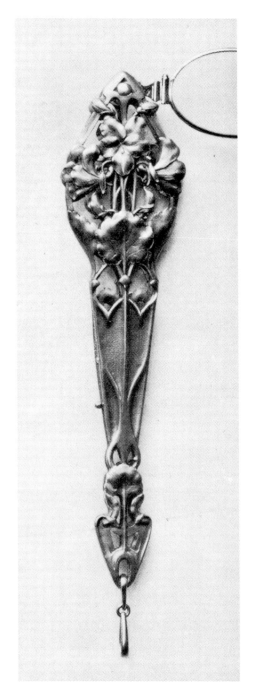

FIG. A   FIG. B

A. *Lorgnon in Chased Gold and Chrysoprase*
    Designed by CAUVIN

B. *Lorgnon in Chased Gold*
    Designed by L. HIRTZ

Executed by BOUCHERON

Fig. B

Fig. C

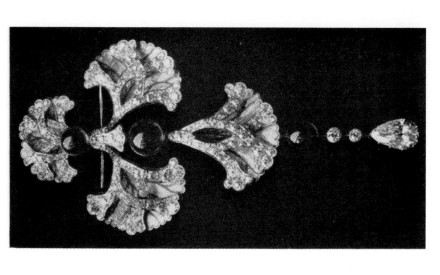

Fig. A

Executed by BOUCHERON

A.   Devant de Corsage, Brilliants upon green Enamel with Emeralds "en cabochon"

B.   Necklet in Chased Gold, with a large Topaz

Both designed by L. HIRTZ

C.   Pendant in Gold, Diamonds, Pearl, Opal and Enamel

VEVER

PLATE 13   FRENCH

FIG. A

FIG. B

A. *Waist-band Buckle in Silver*
   Designed by PAUL RICHARD.   Executed by F. V. ÉDITEUR

B. *Brooches in Chased Gold*
   Designed by L. HIRTZ.   Executed by BOUCHERON

FIG. A   FIG. B

FIG. C   FIG. D

Chatelaines and Watches
F. V. ÉDITEUR and PAUL RICHARD
B and *C* designed by E. BECKER

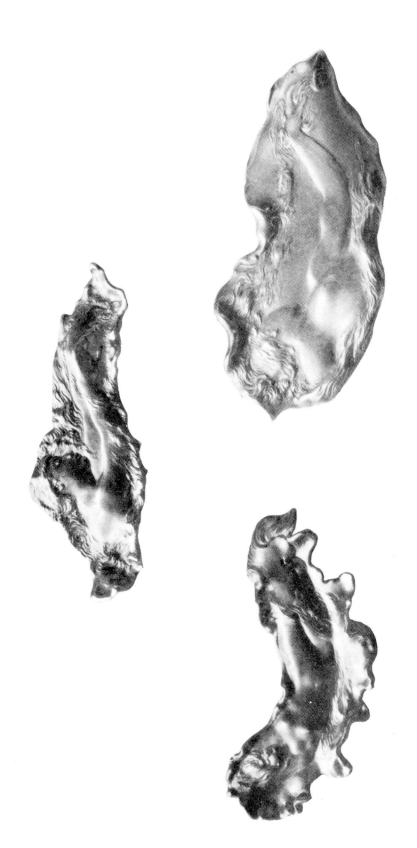

Brooches in Chased Gold JULES DESBOIS

Pendant and Necklet
E. GRASSET

Comb in Enamel, Gold, Shell,
and Precious Stones

Designed by PAUL FOLLOT
Executed by LA MAISON MODERNE

Design for a Comb in Enamel,
Shell, and incrusted Gold

From an original drawing by
HENRI VEVER

Comb in Enamel, Shell, and
Precious Stones

Designed by PAUL FOLLOT
Executed by LA MAISON MODERNE

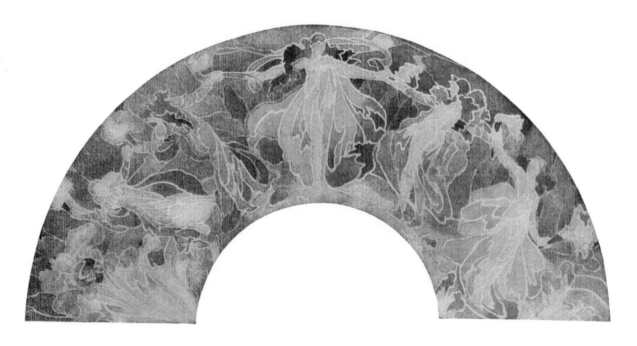

Design for a Stencilled Fan
REGINALD T. DICK

"The Court of Love"
Design for a Painted Fan
H. GRANVILLE FELL

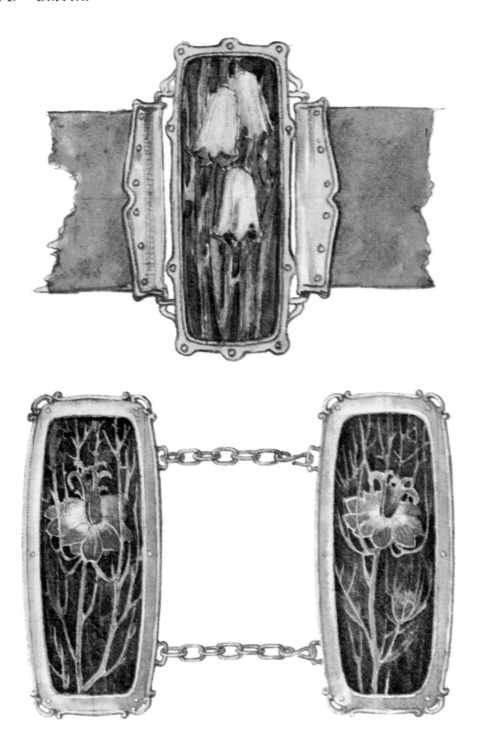

Buckle in Wrought Silver and Enamel
NELSON and EDITH
DAWSON

*Designs for Jewellery in Gold, Silver, Enamels,
Mosaic and Precious Stones*
THOMAS A. COOK

*Enamelled
Silver Brooch*
A. E. ARSCOTT

*Silver Pendant
touched with Enamel*
E. MAY BROWN

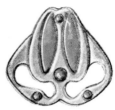

*Enamelled
Silver Brooch*
W. HODGKINSON

*Silver Brooch with
Beads of Enamel*
ANNIE MCLEISH

*Brooch in Silver
and Enamel*
KATE ALLEN

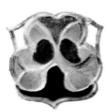

*Silver Locket
Enamelled*
W. HODGKINSON

*Silver Brooch set
with Red Coral*
ISABEL. MCBEAN

*Brooch in Gold
and Enamel with
Pearl Centre*
KATE ALLEN

*Brooch, Silver
and Enamel*
A. E. ARSCOTT

*Silver Brooch enriched
with Enamel*
ANNIE MCLEISH

*Enamelled
Silver Brooch*
W. HODGKINSON

*Brooch in Silver
and Enamel*
DAVID VEAZEY

*Gold Pendant with
Pearls, and Turquoise,
and Champlevé Enamel*
DOROTHY HART

*Brooch in Silver,
Enamel, and
Precious Stones*
B. J. BARRIE

*Gold Pendant
enriched with Enamel*
E. LARCOMBE

*Brooch in Silver
and Enamel*
ANNIE MCLEISH

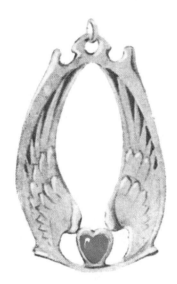

*Silver Pendant
with Enamel*
MINNIE MCLEISH

*Enamelled
Silver Brooch*
MINNIE MCLEISH

*Enamelled Brooch
in Silver*
N. EVERS-SWINDELL

*Brooch in Gold
and Enamel*
M. ALABASTER

*Silver Clasp enriched
with Enamel*
ANNIE ALABASTER

Silver Clasp inset with Enamel
DAVID VEAZEY

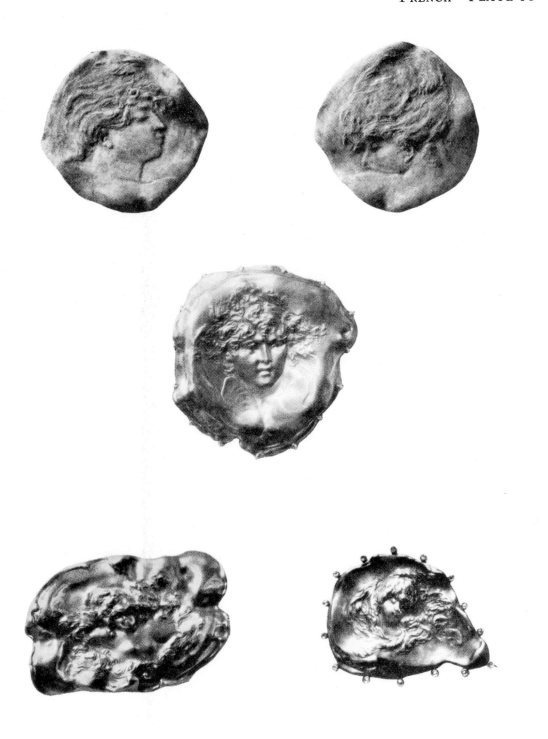

Buttons and Brooches in Chased Gold
JULES DESBOIS

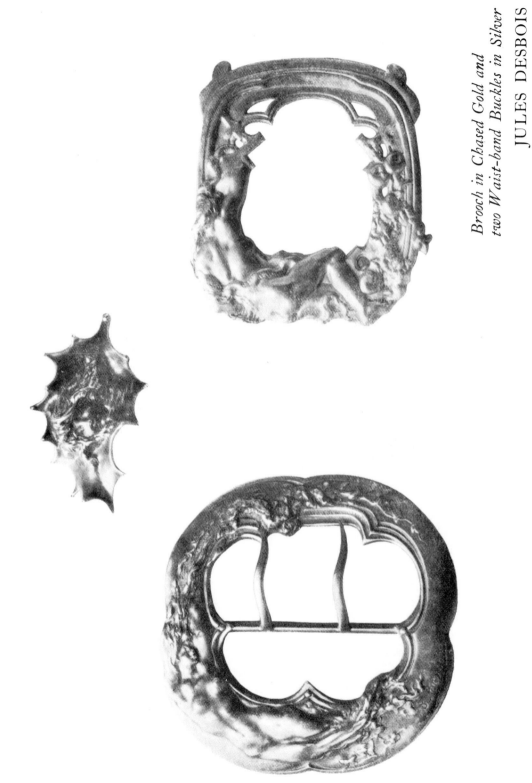

Brooch in Chased Gold and
two Waist-band Buckles in Silver
JULES DESBOIS

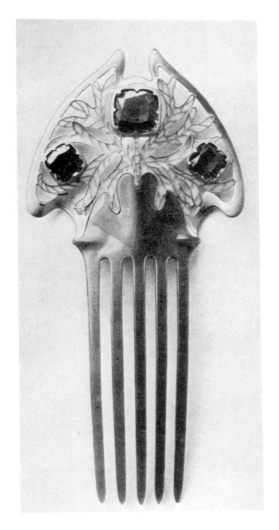

Fig. A

Fig. B

*A.   Comb in Gold and Horn.   Leaves in
    green translucent Enamel, set with
    Siberian Amethysts*

*B.   Horn Fan Handle, incrusted with
    Gold, Brilliants, and Enamel*

VEVER

FIG. B

FIG. A

A. Hat Pins in Gold, Enamel, and Pearl
B. Umbrella Handle, Silver Gilt and Stones
    CH. BOUTET DE MONVEL

26

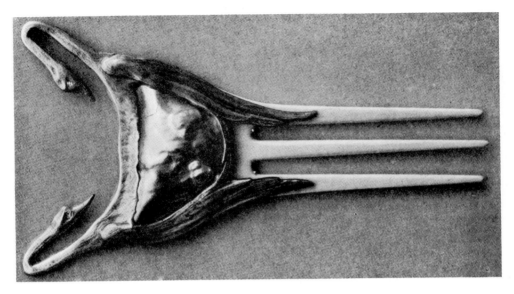

Fig. B

Fig. A

A. *Comb in Horn and Gold with Turquoises*
B. *Comb in Ivory, Silver and Mother-o'-pearl*
CH. BOUTET DE MONVEL

27

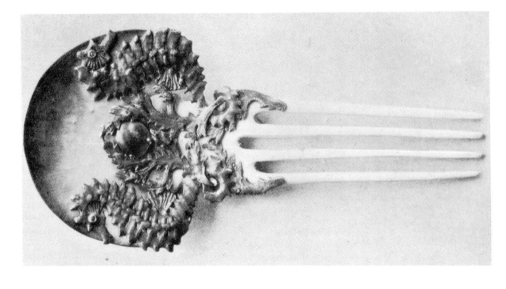

Fig. B

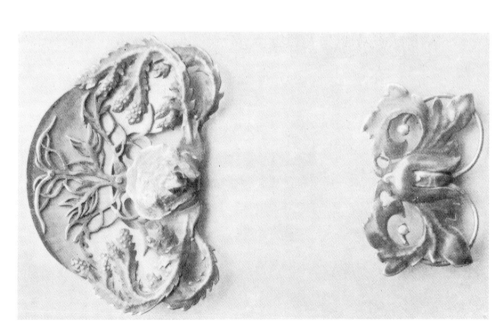

Fig. A

A. *Hammered and Chased Silver Brooches*
B. *Comb in Silver and Mother-o'-pearl*

E. MANGEANT

28

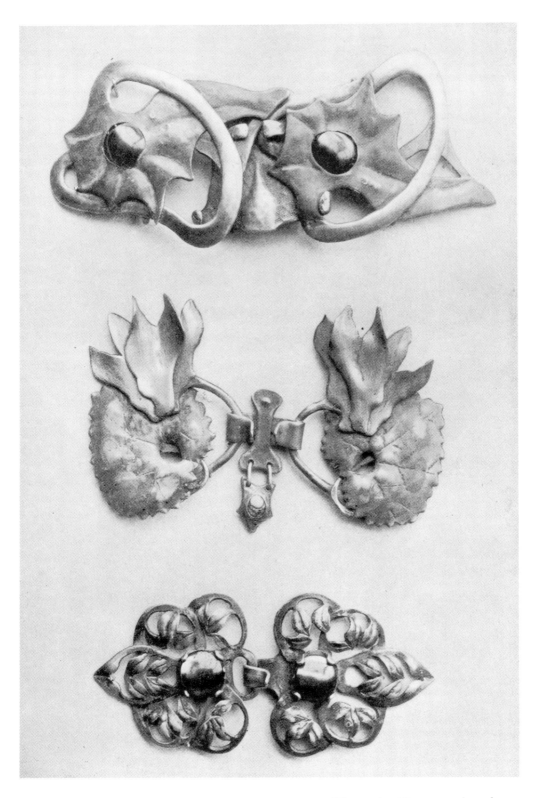

*Clasps in Hammered and
Chased Silver*

E. MANGEANT

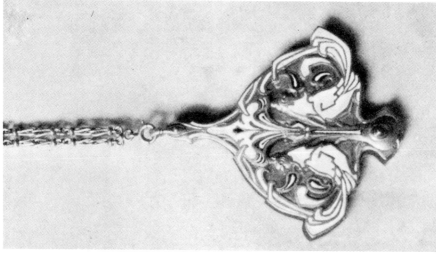

Fig. A

Fig. C

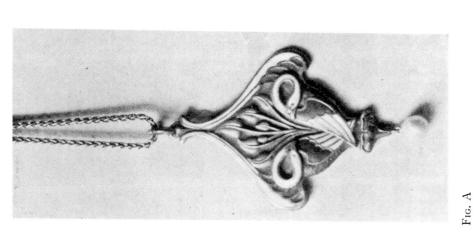

Fig. B

A.   *Pendant in Gold and Enamel*
B.   *Hanging Mirror in Gold and Enamel*
     Designed by MARCEL BING
C.   *Pendant in Gold and Pearls*
     Designed by COLONNA

Executed by *L'ART NOUVEAU*

FIG. A

FIG. B

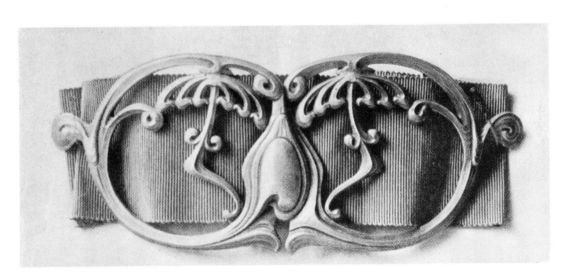

FIG. C

Executed by
L'ART NOUVEAU {

A.   Brooch in Gold, Enamel and Ivory
B.   Pendant in Gold and Enamel

MARCEL BING

C.   Belt Clasp in Gold

COLONNA

PLATE 25   FRENCH

Combs in various materials
Designed by ORAZZI
Executed by LA MAISON MODERNE

FIG. A

FIG. C

FIG. D

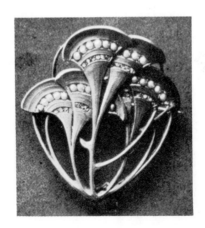

FIG. B

Executed by
LA MAISON MODERNE

*A. & B.   Brooches in Gold with
       Precious Stones*
Designed by M. DUFRÈNE
C.   Comb
Designed by ORAZZI
*D. · Gold Pendant with Enamels
       and Precious Stones*
Designed by P. FOLLOT

PLATE 27   FRENCH

Combs

Designed by ORAZZI

Executed by LA MAISON MODERNE

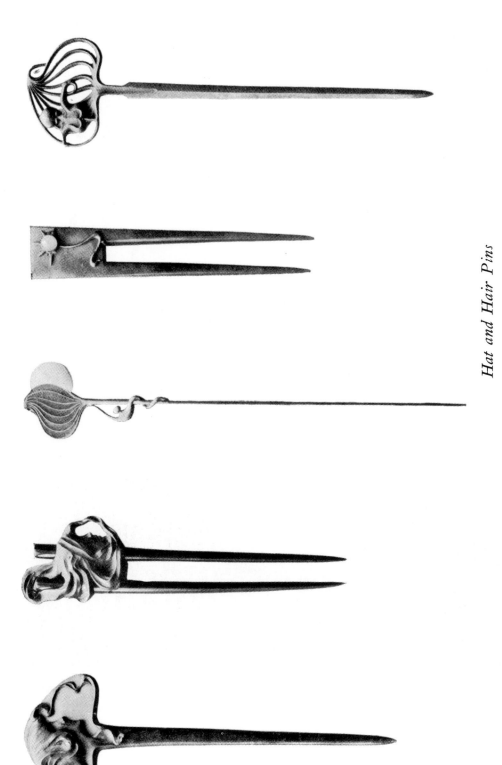

Hat and Hair Pins

Designed by ORAZZI
Executed by LA MAISON MODERNE

35

PLATE 29   FRENCH

FIG. A

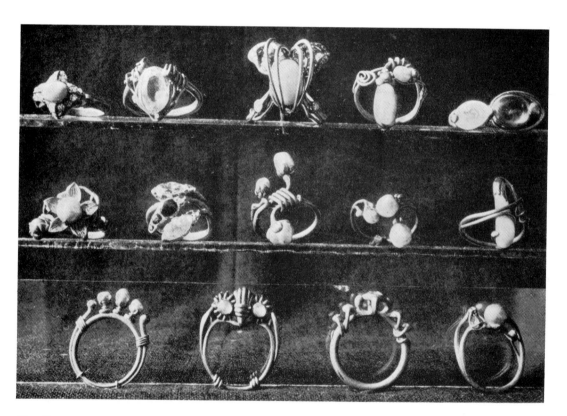

FIG. B

A.   Plaque de Corsage in Gold,
*   Enamel and Precious Stones*
B.   Rings

CHARLES RIVAUD

Silver Waistband Buckles

Designed by TH. LAMBERT
Executed by P. TEMPLIER

PLATE 31   FRENCH

FIG. A

FIG. B

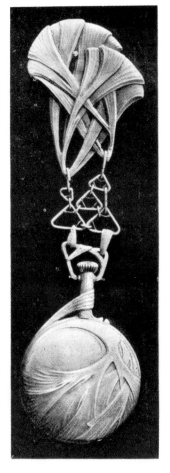

FIG. E

FIG. C

FIG. D

A, B, C & D. Silver Brooches
Designed by TH. LAMBERT
Executed by P. TEMPLIER

E. Chatelaine and Watch
Designed by M. DUFRÈNE
Executed by LA MAISON MODERNE

FIG. A

FIG. B

FIG. C

A & B.   Silver Brooches
C.   Silver Necklet with Pendant

Designed by TH. LAMBERT
Executed by P. TEMPLIER

39

PLATE 33   FRENCH

FIG. A

FIG B

A. *Painted Fan*
    GEORGES DE FEURE

B. *Lace Fan*
    Designed by FÉLIX AUBERT
    Executed by LA MAISON MODERNE

MODERN BRITISH JEWELLERY & FANS. By AYMER VALLANCE.

ONE but the most superficial observers can have failed to note the immense advance that has been attained in British jewellery; though how or at what precise point of time the improvement originated may not be determined with too rash precision. It began not more than fifteen or twenty, nor perhaps later than ten years ago. Somewhere between these two limits is about the approximate date. At any rate, it is certain that, thirty years since, it was quite impossible to procure jewellery in the design and composition of which there entered any artistic taste whatever. Such simply did not exist. Whereas now there is a widespread, though unhappily not a universal, movement amongst us for the design and production of jewellery on true æsthetic principles. The movement may even be described as in a measure concerted, that is, in so far as it presents certain main characteristics common to the work of the various individual artists or schools of artists who are concerned with this branch of decoration.

AND, firstly, must be noted the development of the goldsmith's and silversmith's craft as an important artistic factor entirely distinct and apart from the subsidiary task of stone-setting. The recognition of the art of the metal-worker, as worthy and capable in itself of providing beautiful ornaments, without their serving any such ulterior purpose as sporting trophies or eccentric badges of buffoonery; and also without the adventitious attraction of costly gems, is a decided point gained.

AND, secondly, where stones do happen to be employed, there is an increasing practice of introducing them for the sake of their decorative properties, not, as formerly, for the commercial value they represent in pounds sterling. Mere glitter and the vulgar display of affluence are gradually yielding before the higher considerations of beauty of form and colour. Nor is it any longer deemed improper, should the æsthetic effect of the juxtaposition demand, to set diamonds or other valuable gems side by side with common and inexpensive stones. In these colour combinations, since flash and transparence are become of minor esteem, jewels, instead of being cut in facets, are not infrequently polished in their natural shape, *en cabochon*, or "tallow-cut," as it is called, their irregularities of formation imparting not a little to the barbaric richness of the ornaments in which they occur.

MOREOVER, out of the taste for colour effects in jewellery has arisen an enthusiastic study of the special peculiarities of many gems not hitherto much sought after ; a study resulting in the adoption of certain gems not very precious, yet sufficiently rare, and such that, like Mexican or fire opals, for example, possess peculiar qualities of chameleon-like iridescence or depth or lustre that render them admirably appropriate for quaint and picturesque settings. Among other stones thus employed may be mentioned lapis lazuli ; malachite and its corresponding blue mineral, azurite ; Connemara marble, or serpentine ; amazonite, a light green spar ; chrysoprase ; and lumachella, Hungarian both in name and origin. The last named consists of fossilised shells imbedded in a black matrix, the shells of wonderful iridescence, or flecked with streaks of vivid colour, and possessing, in short, such ornamental qualities as amply compensate the difficulty of obtaining it and of working when obtained. Another material included in the same category is river pearl, or mother-of-pearl, in the form technically known as pearl "blisters," that is, pearls undeveloped in the shell and misshapen, which nevertheless are peculiarly useful for decorative jewellery. One advantage of these substances is that, on account of their comparative cheapness, one does not scruple to diminish and divide and fashion them as may best serve the purpose in hand ; whereas in the case of the more precious stones, like diamonds, whose cost, *ceteris paribus,* increases proportionately with their size and weight, one shrinks from impairing their commercial value, and consequently is apt to preserve them whole, very often at the sacrifice of decorative effect. The craftsman is unhampered in the use of those jewels only which he knows he is at liberty to treat as adjuncts subordinated to his art.

THERE has, moreover, taken place an extended revival of enamelling, an art which offers abundant opportunities for the exercise of the decorator's skill and fancy. It is worthy of remark that our artists' imagination in jewellery seldom degenerates into any great extravagance. For the most part the designs, even among beginners and students in art schools, a number of whom have taken up this branch of ornament, are strictly restrained within bounds, in accord, may be, with our national character of reserve. Few drawings comparatively have been executed, but there is no reason why a large proportion should not be translated from paper into actual existence; for they are in general fairly simple, straightforward, and practicable, or such that, with but slight modifications, could be rendered quite practicable for working purposes.

IT is often stated that art can only flourish through the patronage of the wealthy, to whose comfort and luxury it ministers. If this be true at all, then surely of all things in the world the jeweller's craft should be a case in point, whereas it is conspicuously the reverse. The artistic jewellery produced in this country has not, from its very nature, appealed chiefly to the richest classes of the community, but rather to those of quite moderate means. And while, on the one hand, it is encouraging to observe how much of good work has been and is being done towards raising the standard of jewellery design amongst us, it is nevertheless disappointing to have to record how little support it has found in influential and official quarters. One notable exception is the commission Mr. Alfred Gilbert received to design a mayoral collar, chain and badge for the Corporation of Preston. The sketch model for the same was exhibited at the Royal Academy in 1888, and, for bold originality of outline, as well as for the crisp curling treatment of the parts executed in sheet metal, must have been, as was remarked at the time, a revelation to the ordinary trade jeweller.

AMONG pioneers of the artistic jewellery movement, Mr. C. R. Ashbee holds an honourable place. He stood almost alone at the beginning, when he first made known the jewellery designed by him, and produced under his personal direction by the Guild and School of Handicraft in the East End. It was immediately apparent that here was no tentative nor half-hearted caprice, but that a genuine and earnest phase of an ancient craft had been re-established. Every design was carefully thought out, and the work executed with not less careful and consistent technique. In fact, its high merits were far in advance of anything else in contemporary jewellery or goldsmith's work. The patterns were based on conventionalised forms of nature, favourite among them being the carnation, the rose, and the heartsease, or on abstract forms invited by the requirements and conditions of the material— the ductility and lustre of the metal itself. Most of the ornaments were of silver, the surface of which was not worked up to a brilliantly shining burnish, in the prevalent fashion of the day, but dull polished in such wise as to give the charming richness and tone of old silverwork. Mr. Ashbee also adopted the use of jewels, not lavishly nor ostentatiously, but just wherever a note of colour would convey the most telling effect, the stones in themselves, *e.g.* amethysts, amber, and rough pearl, being of no particular value, save purely from the point of view of decoration. Novel and revolutionary as were, at its first appearance, the principles underlying Mr. Ashbee's jewellery work—viz. that the value of a personal ornament consists not in the commercial cost of the materials so much as in the artistic quality of its design and treatment—they became the standard which no artist thenceforward could wisely afford to ignore, and such furthermore that have even in certain quarters become appropriated by the trade in recent times. Mr. Ashbee himself is an enthusiastic student of Benvenuto Cellini, whose treatises he translated, edited, and printed in 1898. But fortunately the influence of Italian style is by no means paramount in Mr. Ashbee's own designs for jewellery, unless indeed the fine and dainty grace which particularly characterises some of his later work is to be attributed to this source. One or two of the necklaces here reproduced are examples of this lighter manner of Mr. Ashbee's, as the two handsome peacock pattern brooches are of his more solid and substantial jewellery ; while, again, the necklace of green malachite, turquoise, and silver, with pendants of grape bunches alternating with vine-leaf and tendril ornaments, occupies an intermediate position midway between the two former classes of his work.

ONE is always glad to welcome an artist who is courageous and firm enough to grapple with the practical difficulties that surround him, and who sets about to reform, where need requires, the native industry of his own neighbourhood. Such is the aim of Mr. and Mrs. Arthur Gaskin. Their home is in a locality where a large amount of very deplorable jewellery is produced ; so deplorable that they determined, if possible, to provide an antidote to the prevailing degradation. And the reason why the vast mass of the trade jewellery manufactured in Birmingham is bad is that in style and outline it is utterly devoid of artistic inspiration, while at the same time it is perfect as concerns mere technique. The pity of it is that such excellent workmanship should be wasted on such contemptible design. Mr. Gaskin, therefore, saw no alternative but to start afresh, reversing the accepted order of things. His plan is to give the foremost care to the design, and only secondly to regard technique ; and so, by keeping design well in advance, executive skill following after, to raise the former to its proper level. Absence of mathematical uniformity is no doubt held to be a blemish in the opinion of the tradesman, but it gives a living and human interest to the work, and a decorative quality which machine-made articles cannot claim to possess. Mr. Gaskin came to the conclusion that it was of little benefit for a draughtsman to make drawings on paper to be carried out by someone else ; studio and workshop must be one, designer identical with craftsman. It is not very many years since Mr. Gaskin, ably seconded by his wife, started with humble, nay, almost rudimentary apparatus, to make jewellery with his own hands ; but the result has proved how much taste and steadfast endurance can accomplish. Their designs are so numerous and so varied—rarely is any single one repeated, except to order— that it is hardly possible to find any description to apply to all. But it may be noted that, whereas a large number have been characterised by a light and graceful treatment of twisted wire, almost like filigree, the two pendants here illustrated seem to indicate rather a new departure on the part of Mr. Gaskin, with their plates of chased metal, and pendants attached by rings, a method not in any sense copied from, yet in some sort recalling the beautiful fashion with which connoisseurs are familiar in Norwegian and Swedish peasant jewellery.

NEXT in order may be mentioned Mr. Fred Robinson. This artist is actuated by similar ideals as Mr. and Mrs. Gaskin, as is evidenced more especially by his necklace with bent wire pendants of open-work arabesque.

ANOTHER artist of distinction is Miss Annie McLeish, of Liverpool, whose jewellery design, particularly in the way in which the several parts are connected together—an ornamental feature being made out of the structural requirement of strengthening and tying together the portions pierced *à jour*—is curiously suggestive of the perforated iron guards of Japanese sword-handles. At the same time, it is not to be implied that Miss McLeish is at all an imitator of Japanese work. Another point to be noticed is her decorative use of the human figure, in which regard two more lady designers, Miss Larcombe and Miss Winifred Hodgkinson, also excel. The latter, to whose work black-and-white reproduction scarcely does adequate justice, is stronger in her figure work than in that which comes easiest to most people—to wit, the treatment of floral forms that constitute the subordinate portions of the design.

THE number of ladies who have achieved success in jewellery design proves this, indeed, to be a craft to which a woman's light and dainty manipulation is peculiarly adapted. Besides those already mentioned one has only to instance Miss Ethel Hodgkinson and Miss Swindell, who both contribute graceful designs for hat-pins and other small articles ; Miss Dorothy Hart, whose charming *pentacol* is executed by herself ; Miss Kate Fisher and Miss McBean, in whose designs for clasps, etc., enamel is a prominent item ; Miss Alabaster, whose beautiful gold brooch, adorned with blue and green enamel, is based on a *motif* of trees with intertwining stems and roots ; and Miss Rankin, whose four silver hat-pins of handsome design, representing a peacock, thistles, and Celtic beasts respectively, are executed by Mr. Talbot, of Edinburgh, himself a designer as well as artificer. Miss Edith Pickert, in her designs for various articles of jewellery, usually employs a fairly thick outline of metal to enclose a coloured enamel surface. How diversely one and the same *motif* may be rendered in different hands is illustrated by a comparison of Miss Pickert's belt design and Mr. Nelson Dawson's belt-clasps, both in enamel and both founded on the flower "love in a mist."

MR. NELSON DAWSON, well known as an eminent metal-worker and active member of the Society of Arts and Crafts, is also Director of the Artificers' Guild. Another belt-clasp from his design represents the delicate form of the harebell plant.

MR. EDGAR SIMPSON, of Nottingham, is an artist of great gifts, as his drawings and, still more, the specimens of his actual handiwork here illustrated fully testify. Many excellent designs lose vigour and character in the process of execution from the original sketch ; but Mr. Simpson, on the contrary, manages to give his designs additional charm by the exquisite finish with which he works them out in metal. Particularly happy is this artist's rendering of dolphins and other marine creatures ; as in the circular pendant where the swirling motion of water is conveyed by elegant curving lines of silver, with a pearl, to represent an air-bubble, issuing from the fish's mouth.

MR. DAVID VEAZEY'S work, including, among other things, a hair-comb decorated with enamel, has a variegated opal-tinted quality of colour ; while Miss Barrie obtains admirable effects in translucent enamel without backing, after the Russian method. Her design for a belt-clasp with interlaced ornament and stones is excellent. Other belt-clasps and buckles are from designs by Mr. Oliver Baker. Some of this strap-work ornament looks as though it might have been produced by casting from a model ; but, as a matter of fact, it is entirely wrought and folded by hand.

MR. AND MRS. McNAIR'S jewellery, as well as that of Mr. and Mrs. Mackintosh, has that quaint mannerism which one instinctively associates with the Glasgow school of decorators, as also, in a still more marked degree, that of Mr. Talwyn Morris, whose characteristic book-covers are well known. For jewellery, he frequently elects to work in aluminium. His design is strikingly original in effect, though on analysis it is found to consist of very simple units, such as various-sized rectangles overlaid, their boundary lines interpenetrating ; with the occasional apparition of a peacock's eye-feather or the bird's neck and head in the midst. In these cases a completer sense of organic unity might be obtained if, instead of a detached limb, the whole bird were represented, or some other logical coherence established between the incidents of the composition. MR. THOMAS COOK, of West Ham, inserts small slabs of mosaic, after the Italian mode, only he frankly adopts a purely conventional treatment, wisely refraining from any approach to pictorial realism.

IT is a hopeful sign that in many of the technical art schools throughout the land students are taking up jewellery design, and not only that, but in some cases carrying out the actual work themelves. It is largely due to the same fostering influence that the beautiful art of enamelling, frequently referred to above, has been developed amongst us, notably at the Central School of Arts and Crafts, where classes for this department were inaugurated under the able guidance of Mr. Alexander Fisher. But if the improvement in jewellery is to be general and permanent, in order to set it on a secure basis the motive power must come from within. Much good, therefore, may be expected to result from the official sanction afforded by the Goldsmiths' Company to the jewellery work of their Technical Institute, to which a number of very creditable designs owe their existence. Among others may be singled out some decorations for watch-backs, a branch of the craft as useful as it is neglected ; those who have taken it up, like Miss Kate Allen, for instance, being unfortunately but rare exceptions. There is no reason, however, why everyone who carries a watch should not enjoy in it the constant companionship of a thing of beauty.

TO sum up, then, if our modern art jewellery cannot boast any conspicuously brilliant features, at any rate it is of a high average standard. And though, as is the case of all good work, it must needs share many qualities in common with the noble treasures of the past, it yet does not assimilate to any historic style. In fine, it is original ; and, withal, there may be traced in most of it a certain family likeness. It seems almost as if some new-born idea were really beginning to dominate it with the impress of a distinct nationality, destined to develop some day into a tradition which future generations may justly feel it a privilege to follow.

THE case of fans is the exact opposite to that of jewellery. In the former department, it cannot be said that there exists any sort of consensus of ideals, nor any paramount type of ornament. And, notwithstanding the existence amongst us of some few fan-painters of very considerable repute, their operations remain as yet quite personal and individualistic. They have no regular following; have founded no school of decoration. It is, therefore, a subject still open to determine by what principles the ornament of fans should be guided.

FIRSTLY should be taken into account the peculiar shape of the surface available for decoration; and, secondly, the fact that this surface is not a flat plane, but such that must in practice infallibly be broken into so many set divisions or folds. The latter circumstance is the real crux of the question, many decorations, otherwise beautiful enough in the flat, being utterly ruined in effect as soon as they undergo the ordeal of mounting. Thus it may perhaps seem an ingenious plan to subdivide the space horizontally, but it must be remembered that every horizontal line will lose its value when converted, as it must be, into a series of irregular zigzags. The folding is an essential factor, without taking which into account no fan decoration can be satisfactory. In setting out the design, then, it should always be borne in mind that no sharply defined straight lines are admissible, except those that radiate from the centre; and that, of curves, concentric ones are the best, such, that is, as are parallel with the arc shape. If the ornament is floral, it may take the form either of a powdering, or of an all-over pattern of moderately small scrolls. Those on a large scale would run counter to the folds in too emphatic a manner to be agreeable. In figure subjects, of course, care should be taken so to dispose them that no important feature like an eye or a nose be split asunder by the lines of the folds. The larger and more pronounced the pattern, the more necessary it is to observe these conditions. On the other hand, where the colouring is of fairly even tone, and without strongly contrasted masses, or where the design is on a small scale, the surface can the more safely be spaced out by lines or medallions or cartouches, or other devices that may commend themselves.

AS regards material, there is no question that a silk ground, prepared with rice-size and stretched, until the decoration is completed, on a stretcher, offers as suitable a texture as one could desire for delicate and softly-blended harmonies in water-colour; as the fans of Mr. Conder, a prolific fan-painter, whose work appeals to a large circle of admirers, amply testify. The detail is all Mr. Conder's own, though the influence of French XVIIIth century ornament is unmistakable.

MISS SYRETT again is a clever artist working on somewhat similar lines. No one, however, who knew her figure compositions in her Slade School days, productions full of promise, if marred by the attenuated model with prim, smooth-drawn hair, the type of Carlos Schwabe's illustrations to " Le Rêve " and "l'Évangile," could have foreseen that Miss Syrett would develop in the direction of her present work. The reduced black-and-white illustrations convey no idea of the tender beauty of the colouring, nor of the exquisite pen-work in brown with which such features as the faces, hair, and hands are executed.

ANOTHER gifted artist is Mr. Brangwyn, who now makes his *début* as a fan decorator, with a finished painting on silk, and also a crayon study for the same purpose. His design shows how much individuality an artist may impart even to work consciously founded on that of a past style. Here, for example, in the drawing of Cupids shooting their darts at a pair of lovers, may be recognised the very figures of the Trianon period, but happily without any of their doll-like affectation and effeminacy.

THOSE who recollect Miss Jessie King's drawing in the last winter's special number of THE STUDIO—her *Pelleas and Mélisande* —in which the lank forms of Schwabe or Toorop were combined with a wealth of accessory ornament of the artist's own, will scarcely recognise her hand in the present fan. She seems to be able to pass with marvellous facility from one fully matured style to another. The elaborate, nay, luxuriant finish of the whole, to say nothing of separate details such as the butterflies, the festoons, knots, etc., vividly recall the work of the late Aubrey Beardsley. It is no derogation of Miss King's remarkable powers to assert that, but for the existence of Mr. Beardsley, this drawing of hers would certainly not have been what it is. One could wish that, for the sake of support to the leaf, more room had been allowed to the sticks. But, apart from this defect, the dainty care with which every minute detail is consistently carried out merits little else than praise.

MISS CHRISTINE ANGUS contributes two designs—one, in a pictorial style, for a paper fan, not nearly so decorative as the other, of nude boys and sweet peas, for painting on silk. Miss Ethel Larcombe's gauze fans are attractive compositions, which bear tokens of a diligent appreciation of Granville Fell.

ANOTHER kind of fan ornamentation is exemplified by the stencil work of Mr. Reginald Dick and Mr. Thomas Cook. It is true these decorations are in a degree, but only in a slight degree, mechanical. The one unchangeable element is the white tie-lines of the pattern. For the rest, no little skill is required of the artist in devising and cutting his stencil. The number of plates is limited, but the mode adopted of colouring by hand admits of such variations that no two specimens from the identical stencil plates would ever be alike. Mr. Dick's fan is provided with enamelled sticks in keeping with the other parts of the decoration. Mr. Cook's design is the less characteristic of this particular method. Indeed, though finished off at either end with a certain plausibility, the pattern is an obvious repeat, and such that might very well be the section of a circular dish border.

LESS ambitious are the designs for different sorts of lacework by Miss Hammett and Miss Naylor. Each of these patterns, while keeping strictly within the limits of the special technique proposed, shows yet much freshness and fertility of resource. In the one case the design is floral, in the other the theme is relieved by the introduction of bird forms into the composition.

TO conclude, the scope for decoration that fans afford is so great, and the possible methods so manifold, that the wonder is there are not many more artists employed in this industry. It is one well worthy of their attention ; and it is to be hoped that no long time may elapse before the joint efforts of designers may, in this, as already in other branches of arts and crafts, result in something like a native style of ornamentation being evolved.

AYMER VALLANCE.

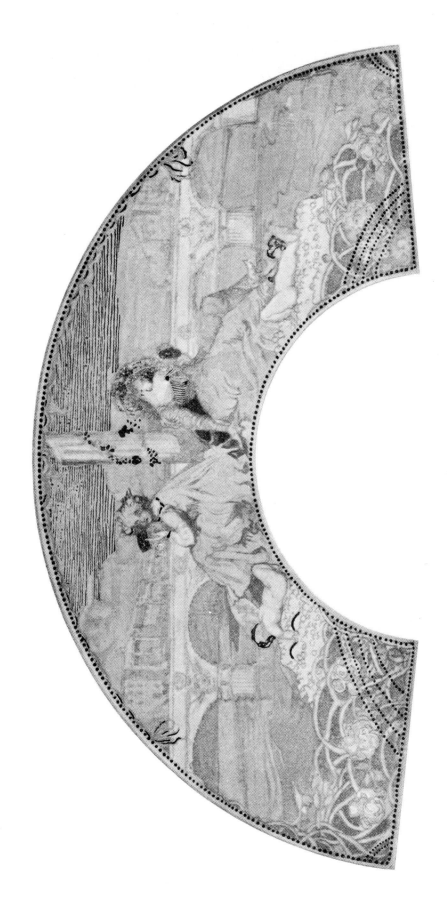

A Fan Painted on Silk
FRANK CONDER
(*In the possession of Thomas Greg, Esq.*)

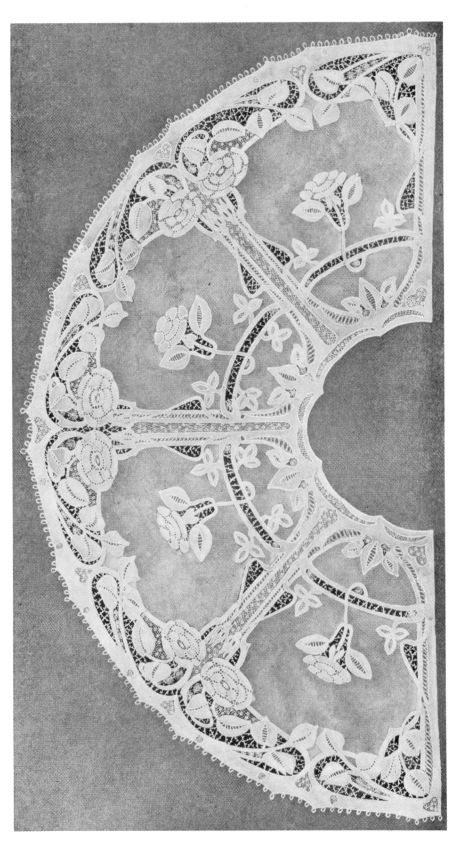

Design for a Lace Fan MYRA NAYLOR

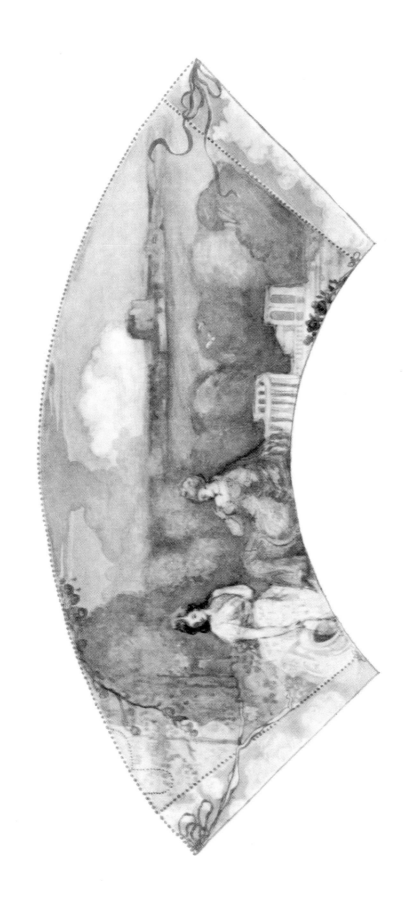

A Fan Painted on Silk
FRANK CONDER
(In the possession of Dalhousie Young, Esq.)

Fig. A

Fig. B

A. " The Medallion" Fan
B. " A Travesty" Fan

FRANK CONDER

(By permission of Messrs. Carfax & Co.)

55

PLATE 39   BRITISH

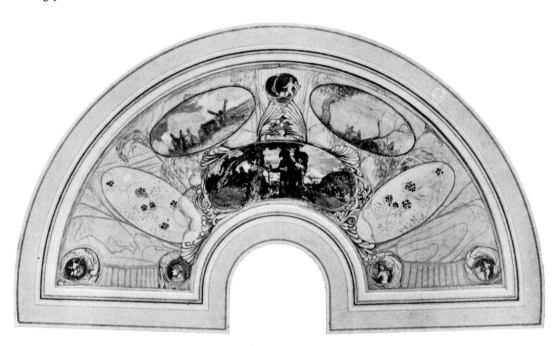

FIG. A

FIG. B

A. " The Empire " Fan
B. " L'Anglaise " Fan
FRANK CONDER

(By permission of Messrs. Carfax & Co.)

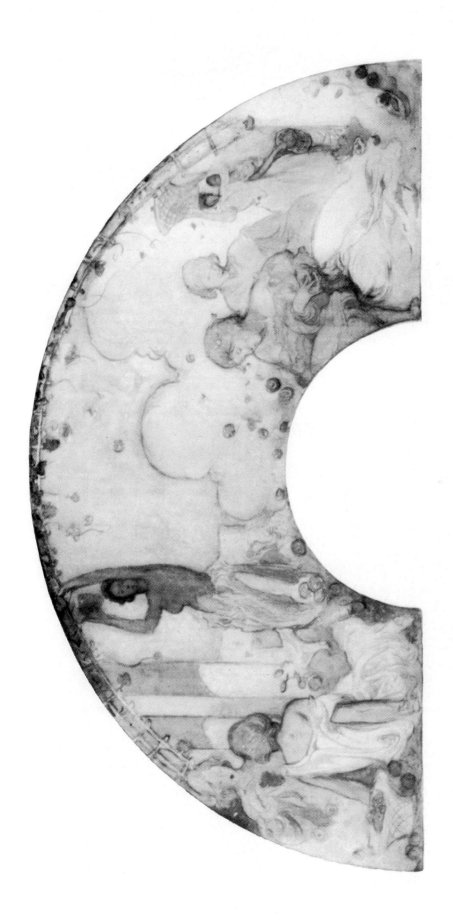

A Painted Silk Fan
FRANK   BRANGWYN

PLATE 41   BRITISH

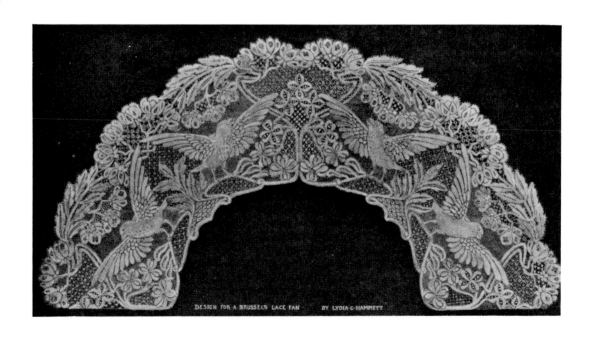

Designs for Lace Fans
LYDIA C. HAMMETT

58

Designs for Painted Gauze Fans
ETHEL LARCOMBE

PLATE 43   BRITISH

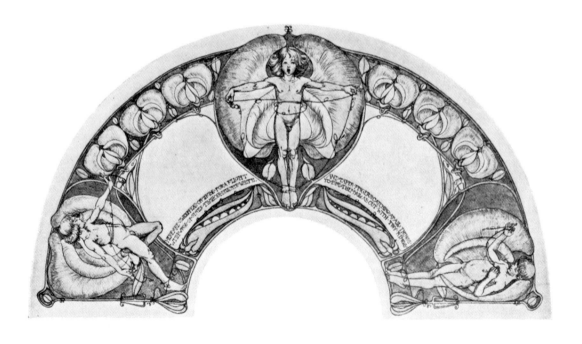

Designs for Painted Silk Fans
CHRISTINE ANGUS

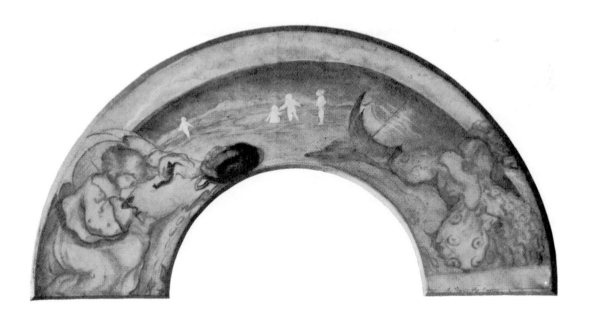

Painted Silk Fans

NELLIE SYRETT

PLATE 45   BRITISH

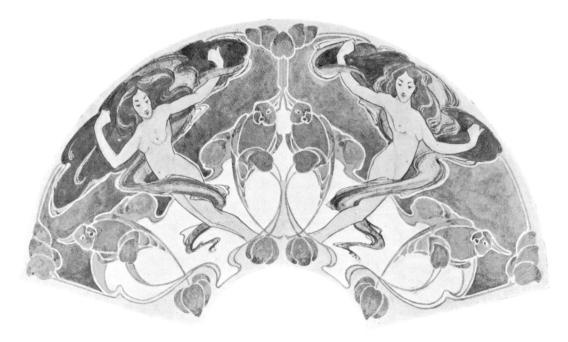

FIG. A

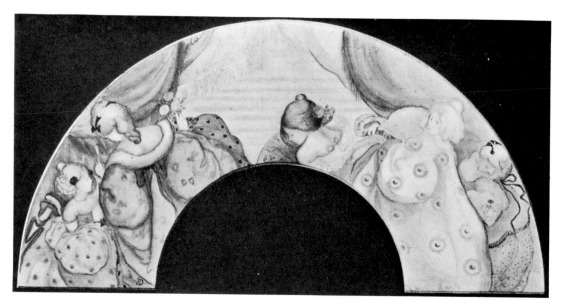

FIG. B

A.   Painted Silk Fan
THOMAS A. COOK

B.   Painted Silk Fan
NELLIE SYRETT

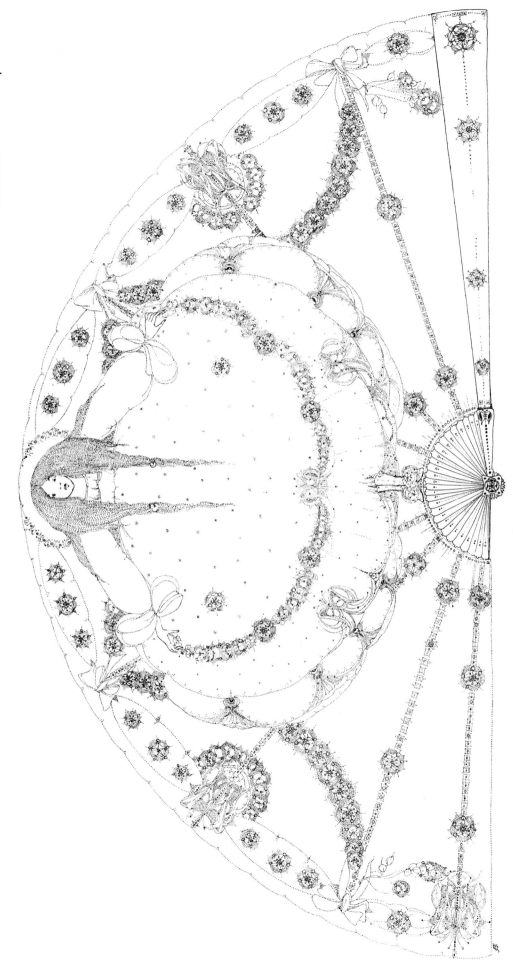

Design for a Fan JESSIE M. KING

FIG. B

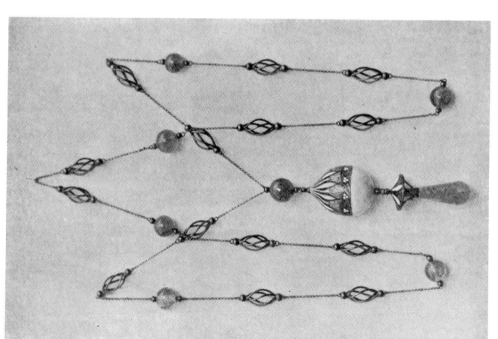

FIG. A

A. Necklet in Gold and Silver, with Amethysts and Enamels
B. Necklet in Silver and Gold, green Malachite and Turquoise

Designed by C. R. ASHBEE
Executed by THE GUILD OF HANDICRAFT

64

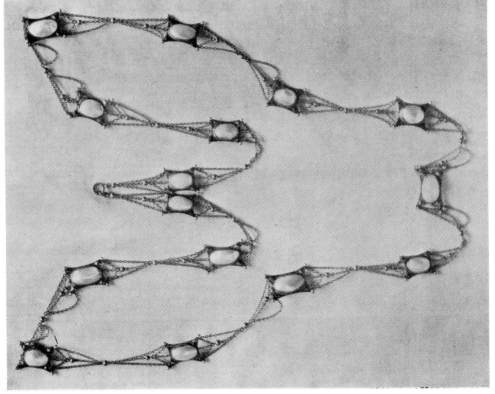

FIG. B

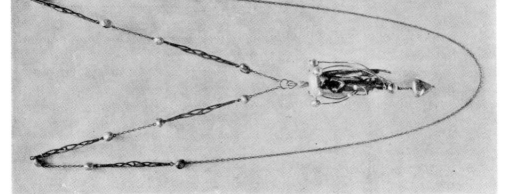

FIG. A

A. *Necklet in Gold, Pearls and Enamels*
B. *Silver Muff-Chain with Pearl Blisters*

Designed by C. R. ASHBEE
Executed by THE GUILD OF HANDICRAFT

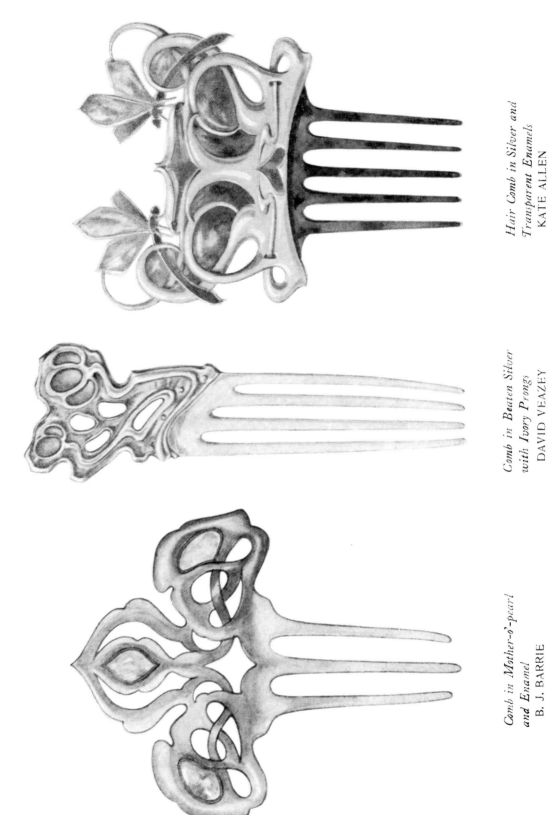

Hair Comb in Silver and
Transparent Enamels
KATE ALLEN

Comb in Beaten Silver
with Ivory Prongs
DAVID VEAZEY

Comb in Mother-o'-pearl
and Enamel
B. J. BARRIE

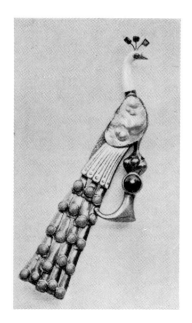

FIG. A

FIG. C

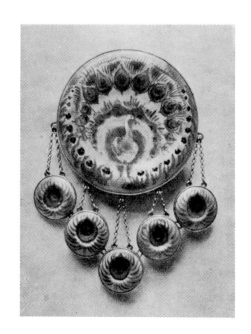

FIG. B

A. Peacock Brooch with Pearls, White Enamel and Turquoises

B. Silver Brooch, with Green and Blue Enamels

C. Peacock Brooch, in Gold, with Pearls and Diamonds, a Ruby in the Peacock's eye

Designed by C. R. ASHBEE

Executed by

THE GUILD OF HANDICRAFT

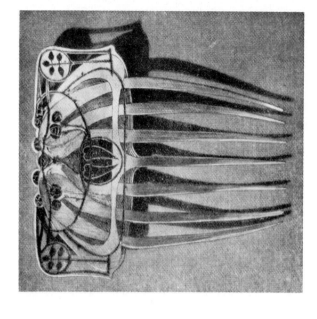

FIG. B

FIG. A

A. *Silver Clasp, enriched with Amethysts, Pearls and pale violet Enamel*
    Designed by C. R. ASHBEE
    Executed by THE GUILD OF HANDICRAFT

B. *Hair Comb, in Silver and Enamels*
    FRANCES McNAIR

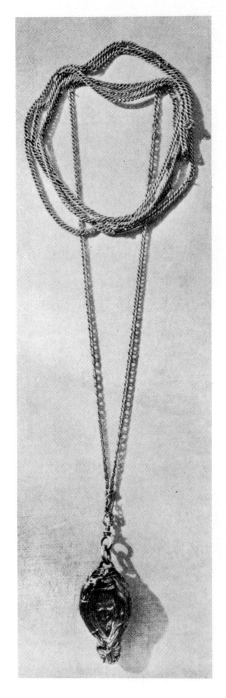

FIG. A   FIG. B

A. *Vinaigrette and Chain*
        J. HERBERT McNAIR

B. *Pendant in beaten Silver,*
    pierced and enamelled to hold
    a Crystal Locket
        FRANCES McNAIR

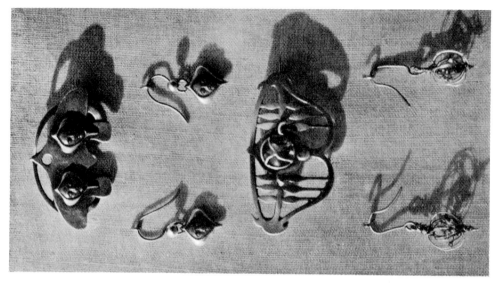

FIG. B

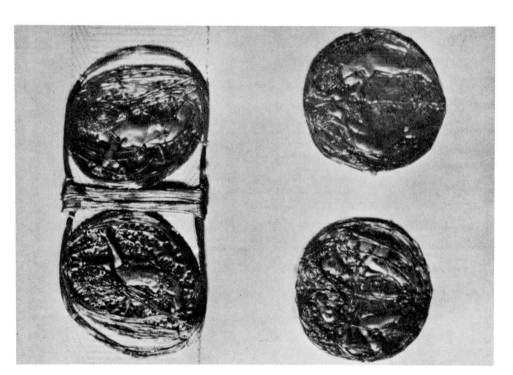

FIG. A

A. *Belt-buckle and two Brooches in beaten Silver and Wire*
B. *Brooches and Earrings*

J. HERBERT McNAIR

FIG. A

FIG. B

A. *Necklace in Gold and Enamel*
   KATE FISHER

B. *Belt in Silver and Enamel*
   EDITH PICKETT

PLATE 55   BRITISH

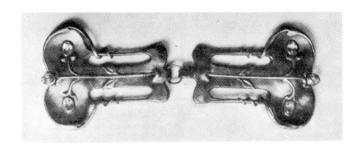

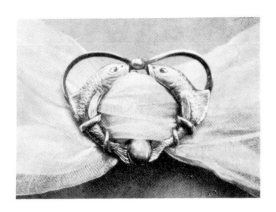

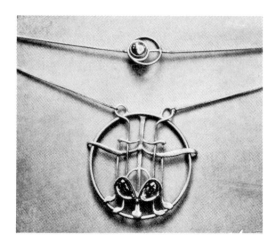

Silver Clasps and Gold Pendants
set with Opals and Amethysts

EDGAR SIMPSON

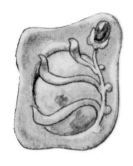
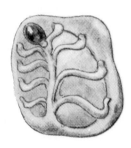
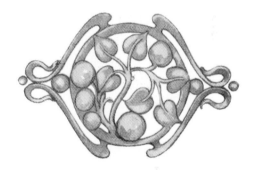

*A Pendant, Two Buttons, a Brooch
and a Cloak Clasp in Silver*
EDGAR SIMPSON

PLATE 57   BRITISH

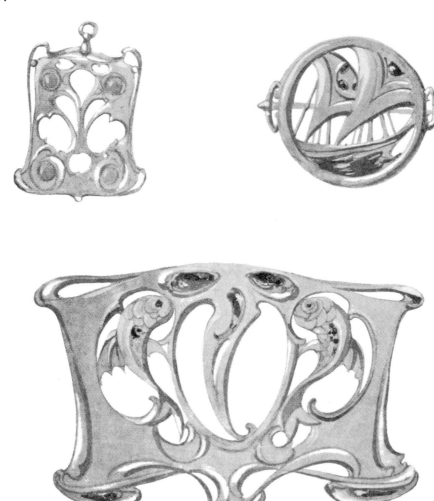

Silver Pendant, Brooch and Clasp
ANNIE McLEISH

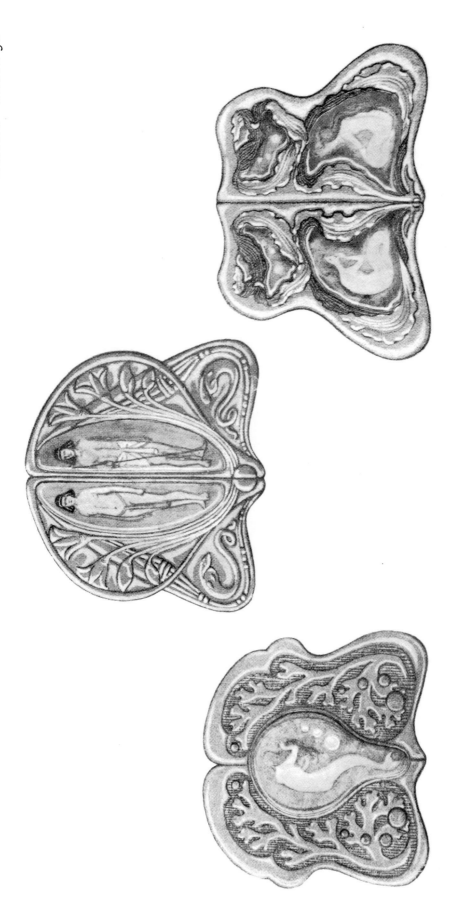

Belt Buckles in Silver, Niello and Enamels

WINIFRED HODGKINSON

PLATE 59   BRITISH

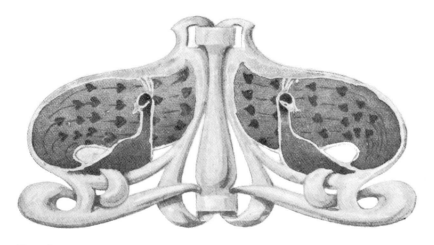

FIG. A

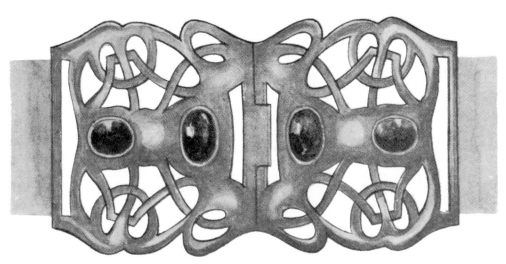

FIG. B

A.   Enamelled Silver Belt-Clasp
KATE ALLEN
B.   Silver Clasp set with Stones
B. J. BARRIE

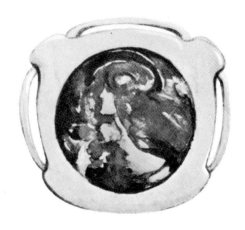

Clasps in Silver and Enamel
ANNIE McLEISH

PLATE 61   BRITISH

Watch Backs in Silver and Enamels
KATE ALLEN

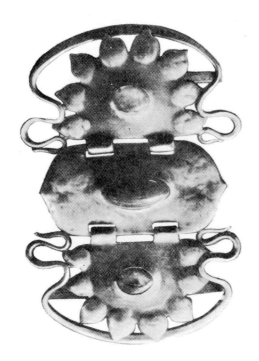

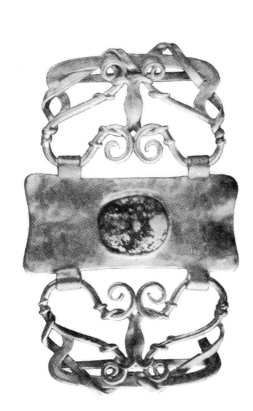

Silver Clasps set with Stones
OLIVER BAKER

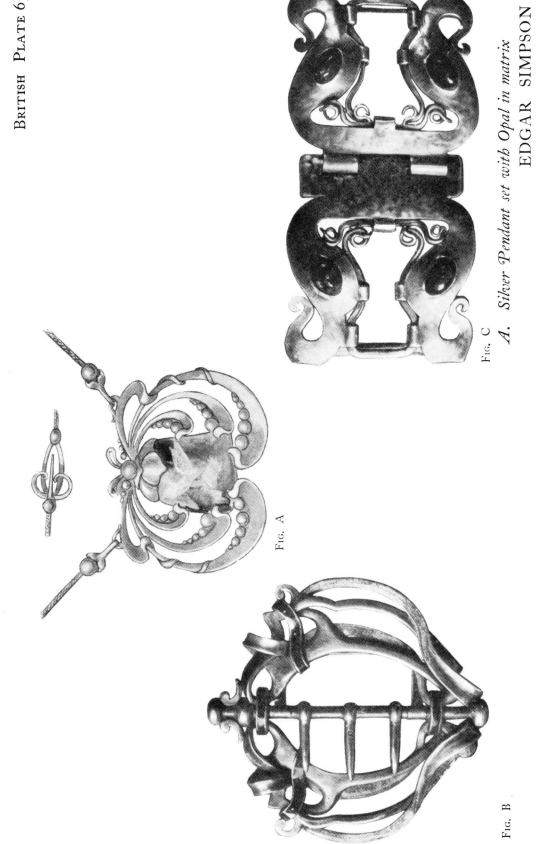

FIG. A

FIG. B

FIG. C

A. *Silver Pendant set with Opal in matrix*
EDGAR SIMPSON

B and C. *Silver Buckles*
OLIVER BAKER

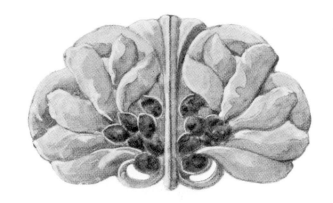

Clasps in Silver and Enamels
KATE FISHER

PLATE 65   BRITISH

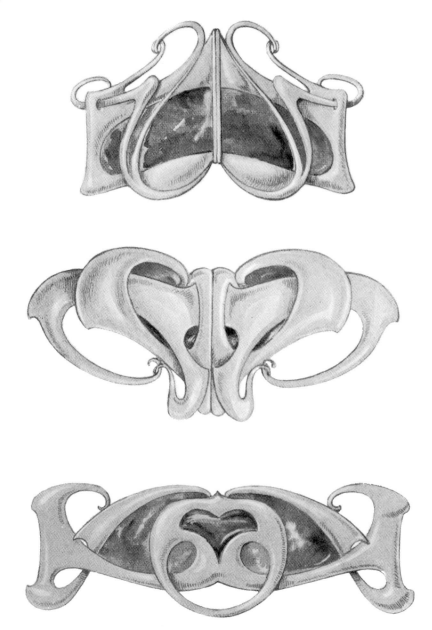

Clasps in Silver and Enamels
KATE ALLEN

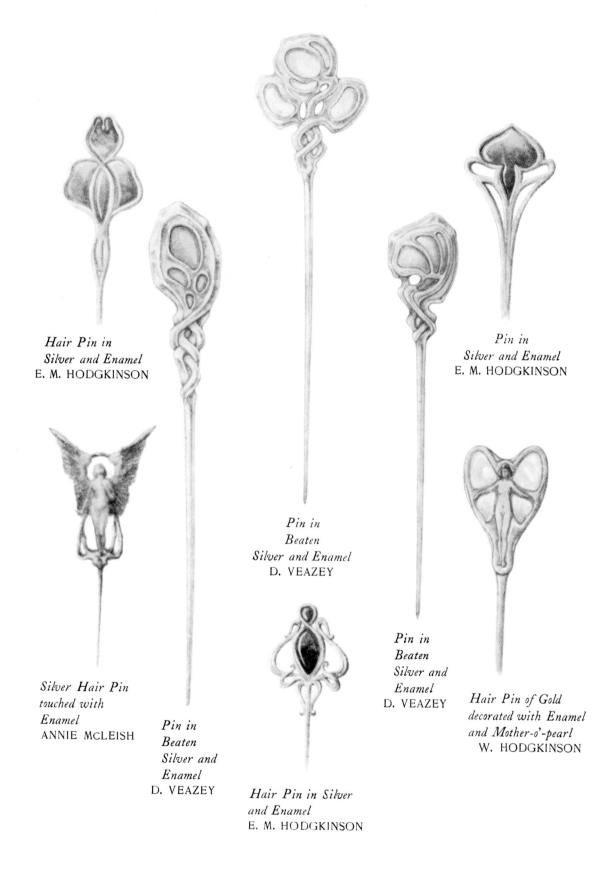

*Hair Pin in
Silver and Enamel*
E. M. HODGKINSON

*Pin in
Silver and Enamel*
E. M. HODGKINSON

*Pin in
Beaten
Silver and Enamel*
D. VEAZEY

*Silver Hair Pin
touched with
Enamel*
ANNIE McLEISH

*Pin in
Beaten
Silver and
Enamel*
D. VEAZEY

*Pin in
Beaten
Silver and
Enamel*
D. VEAZEY

*Hair Pin of Gold
decorated with Enamel
and Mother-o'-pearl*
W. HODGKINSON

*Hair Pin in Silver
and Enamel*
E. M. HODGKINSON

83

PLATE 67   BRITISH

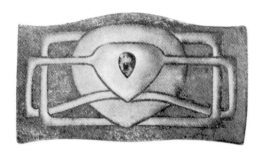

FIG. C

FIG. A

FIG. B

FIG. D

A and B.   Jewelled Brooches in beaten Copper
C and D. · Jewelled Buckles in beaten Aluminium

TALWIN MORRIS

FIG. A

FIG. B

FIG. C

A.   Jewelled Shoe-Buckle in beaten Copper
B.   Cloak Clasp in beaten Silver
C.   Waist-band Clasp in beaten Silver

TALWIN MORRIS

PLATE 69   BRITISH

FIG A

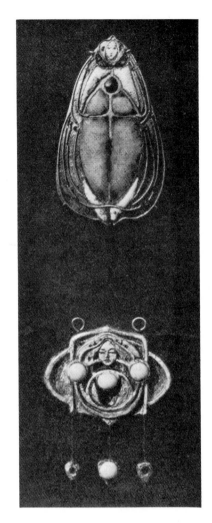

FIG. C

FIG. B

A and B.   Buckles in beaten Aluminium
TALWIN MORRIS

C.   Pendants in Silver; the upper one
with Enamels, the lower with Turquoises
FRANCES McNAIR

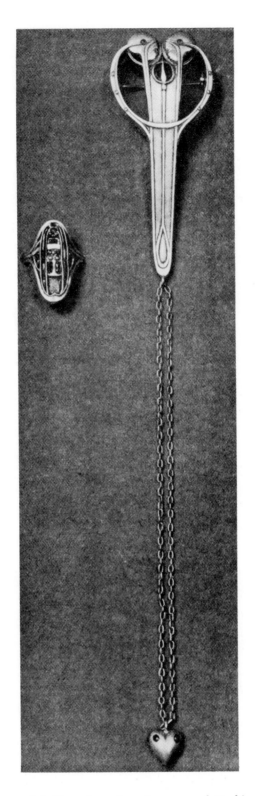

Silver Finger Ring set with Pearls, Amethysts, and Rubies
CHARLES R. MACKINTOSH

Silver Brooch and Pendant Heart set with Rubies, Pearls, and Turquoises
M. MACDONALD MACKINTOSH

PLATE 71   BRITISH

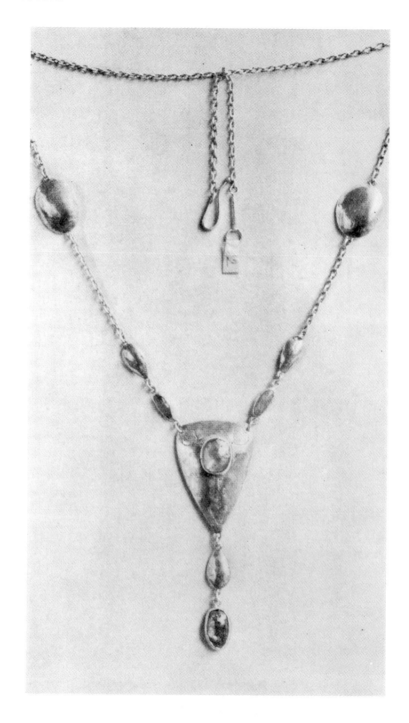

*Necklet of beaten Silver, chased, and
set with Fire Opals*

ARTHUR J. GASKIN

*Silver Pendant and Chain
set with Turquoises and
Chrysoprase*

ARTHUR J. GASKIN

PLATE 73   BRITISH

FIG. A

FIG. B

A. *Silver Belt*
B. *Silver Necklet, set with Pearl Blisters,*
    Coral and Aquamarine

FRED S. ROBINSON

FIG. A

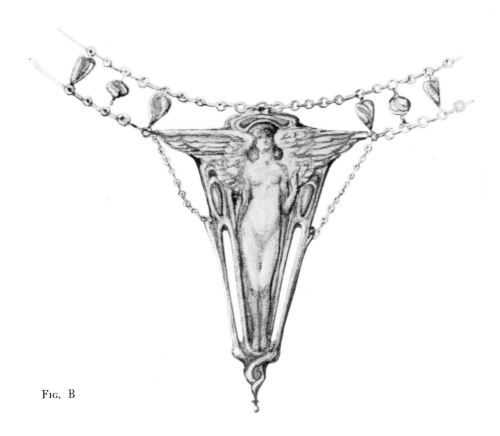

FIG. B

A. Silver Chain and Pendants set with Stones
ISABEL McBEAN
B. Enamelled Silver Pendant
MINNIE McLEISH

PLATE 75   BRITISH

Silver and Enamel Clasps,
Pins and Brooches

EDITH PICKETT

Fig. A

Fig. B

Fig. C

Fig. D

Fig. E

Fig. F

Fig. G

A, D, G.   Brooches and a Cross in Gold, set with Stones
ANNIE McLEISH

B.   Brooch in Silver and Enamels
DAVID VEAZEY

C.   Silver Brooch with Opals
ETHEL M. HODGKINSON

F.   Brooch in Silver, Enamel and Pearls
NORA EVERS-SWINDELL

93

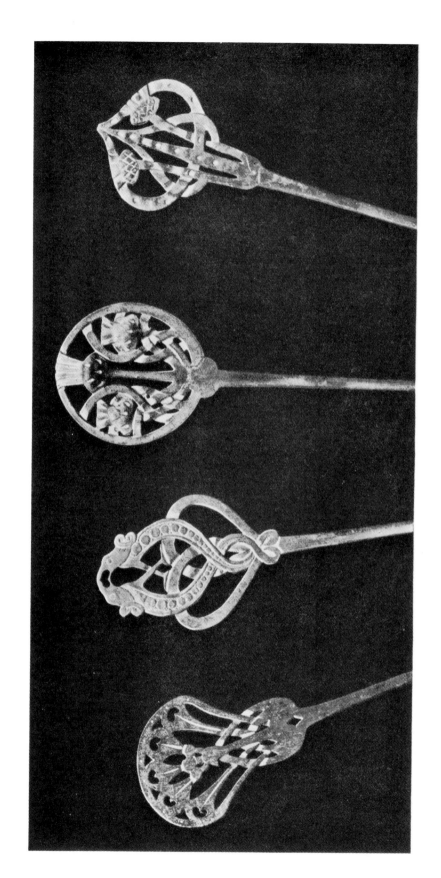

Four Silver Hat Pins

Designed by ARABELLA RANKIN
Executed by J. M. TALBOT

94

Fɪɢ. A

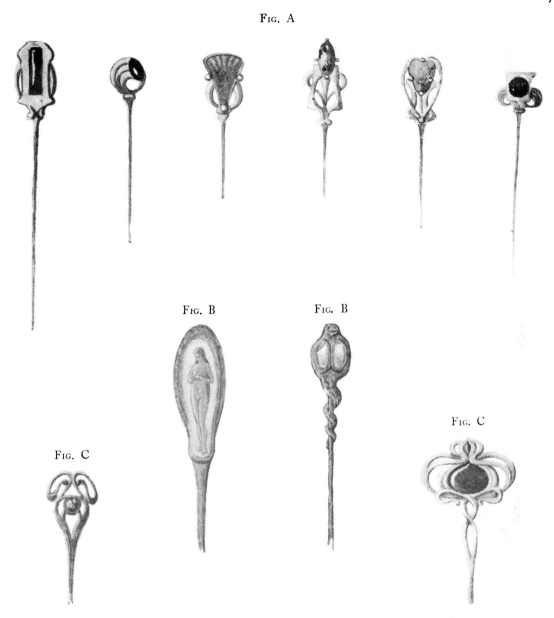

Fɪɢ. B

Fɪɢ. B

Fɪɢ. C

Fɪɢ. C

A.   Six Pins in Silver and Enamel
NORA EVERS-SWINDELL

B.   Two Pins in Silver and Enamel
WINIFRED HODGKINSON

C.   Two Silver Pins set with Enamel
ETHEL M. HODGKINSON

MODERN AUSTRIAN JEWEL-LERY. BY W. FRED.

CRITICAL examination of the jewellery of any particular period cannot fail to be practically a chapter of the history of culture. The popular saying : " Every time has the poet it deserves," is superficially true, yet holds within itself a certain element of falsehood, as does pretty well every commonplace proverb of the same kind. However, if the sentence be slightly modified, as it very well may be, so that it reads, " Every time has the jewellery it deserves," there will be absolutely nothing untrue about it, for the ornaments worn, whether on the dress, the hair, or the person of the wearer, have always reflected in a marked degree the taste of their period, and are very distinctly differentiated from those of any other time, so that changes in fashion imply changes of a more radical description in popular feeling.

A HISTORY of personal ornament is open to many side issues. and unfolds itself in two different—indeed, opposite—directions, Primitive savages, as is well known, wear ornaments before they take to clothes. The Fiji islanders sport gold chains round their necks, and the African negroes in their untamed state load themselves with every glittering object they can get hold of, looking upon the multiplication of ornaments as a sign of wealth. Very different, of course, is the state of civilisation of those who look upon decoration as an evidence of art culture, and care only for such ornaments as require the exercise of technical skill in their production, valuing them in proportion to the amount of that skill displayed by their craftsmen, rather than the intrinsic value of their material. The time of the Italian Renaissance is an instance of the truth of this. As has so often before been the case in the times of transition which are of inevitable recurrence, our own modern epoch is characterised by a certain unrest and confusion, in which many tendencies are contending with each other side by side, and neutralising, to a great extent, each other's effects. In America, the Tiffany company seems to aim at producing masses of precious stones, which will give primarily the impression of the great wealth of their owner and producer; whereas, in France, Lalique the jeweller endeavours rather to throw into the background the actual value of the jewels, their artistic setting being the first thing to strike the observer. We in Austria have greater leanings to France than to America, and precious stones, however great their intrinsic value, are looked upon as of quite secondary value in modern art-work to beauty of line and of colour. French influence on Austrian work cannot fail to be recognised. Its germs fell indeed on a soil of exceptional fertility, with the result that they have taken root and borne abundant fruit. It should perhaps, however, be remarked that those races who are the heirs of a strong art tradition do not need, as do others less fortunate, to prove the wealth of their inheritance by the use of lavish ornament. Their inherent artistic culture is indeed evidenced by the fact that they expect their artists to exercise their skill on materials less costly than do those who, to a certain extent, have their reputations still to make. Benvenuto Cellini had to be content to work in silver, the Americans want to have every stick or umbrella-handle to be of gold.

IF we cast a glance, however hasty and cursory it may be, over the development of jewellery in Vienna, noting the forms most popular in that city in past times, it is impossible not to be struck with the way in which every historical phase of art is reflected in these forms. The favourite style with Viennese jewellers, and that in which the most effective, and at the same time the most characteristic, results have been achieved was undoubtedly the so-called *baroque*, a term originally restricted to a precise architecture or art-style alone, but now loosely applied to characterise any ornamental design of an unusual kind. It is in this half-serious, half-sportive style, with its grotesque yet bold effects and its complete freedom from convention, that the finest pieces of Austrian jewellery have been produced. At the time of the great Congress of Vienna, when the representatives of the Powers met in that city to settle the affairs of Europe after the fall of Napoleon—that is to say, about one hundred years later than the first introduction of the *baroque* style from Italy, French work, though it was of a crude description, exercised an influence over Austrian jewellers, and what seemed like a second renaissance of the art of ornament began in Austria.

THE art of jewellery in Austria remained under French influence almost until the present day—in fact, throughout the whole of the 19th century—and it has only been in the last year that Austrian art-industries have been set free from the foreign yoke which so long oppressed them, so that the true Viennese style of jewellery has but rarely come to the fore. Now at last, however, the liberating influence of the modern spirit is making itself felt in the art of jewellery, as in everything else ; and every ornament produced, whether in precious stones or in enamel, bears the unmistakable impress of the distinctive psychic character of our capital city, which even foreigners do not fail to recognise. The result of this individuality is that a work of art is indissolubly bound up with the personality of its creator, and with the idiosyncrasies of the town which was its birthplace.

IN Austria men wear very little jewellery, and the only noteworthy examples of ornaments made for them which can be quoted are a few rings and charms, the former perhaps adorned with designs in low-relief. The flat gold circle of the wedding-ring, which can be easily carried in the waistcoat pocket, and the engagement-ring, the psychic meaning of which is clear enough, the latter generally bearing one large diamond or other precious stone, do not afford much scope for the æsthetic feeling of their makers. A man who ventures to wear much jewellery is called old-fashioned, but there are still people who dare to sport a single great diamond or some other simple ornament on their shirt fronts. A pearl without setting, an emerald, or so-called sapphire *en cabochon*, are still frequently seen. The present fashion allowing men to tie their cravats in all manner of different styles to suit their own particular fancy, has led to the manufacture of a few varieties of scarf rings which admit of a certain amount of artistic intertwining of the gold, if it be gold of which they are made. When the making of jewellery for men is left to the unfettered imagination of the artist, he generally produces something quaintly original and fantastic, such as queer figurals, grotesque masks, comic caricatures of human or half-human figures or faces, etc.

ON the other hand, there is no doubt that there is far more activity in the production of jewellery for women in Vienna than in almost any other city. The culture of our town is, indeed, essentially feminine. The graceful and witty, yet dreamy and passionate, girls and women of Vienna give to it its distinctive character. A foreigner who once spent two days only in our capital was yet able to say of it, that all through his wanderings in its streets and alleys the rhythm of female culture was sounding in his ears. The men of Vienna pride themselves more than the French, more even than the people of Northern Europe, on their women, and as a result of this pride there is sure to be plenty of beautiful jewellery of varied design to be met with in the town in which they live.

AMONGST jewels and precious stones the spotless white pearl is perhaps the favourite, but, as proved at the last great Exhibition in Paris, the pale rose-coloured coral from the East runs it very close. Diamonds are still set in the old-fashioned way—that is to say, after simple designs, the best of which are copies from Renaissance or *baroque* models. Only now and then is any attempt made to produce lightly incised representations direct from Nature of flowers, birds, or leaves. Of course, bouquets of brilliants and leaves consisting entirely of diamonds have always been easily made at any period ; but what is now aimed at for that very reason is the evolution of designs which shall be essentially true to Nature, but at the same time really artistic. Crude masses of naturalistic flowers are really of no account whatever, for a bouquet of diamonds can never have the exquisite charm of a fresh, sweet-smelling bunch of real blossoms. Only a fairly good design, founded on some flower or leaf which can be satisfactorily reproduced in, and is, so to speak, *en rapport* with, the jewels to be used, can succeed in pleasing through beauty of form alone, independently of any association. Good examples of the best style of ornament in which precious stones are used are the necklace, figured herewith, with the earrings to match, by Roset and Fisch-meister. In them the natural form, which has been the motive from which the design was evolved, was the fruit and leaf of the rare plant known in Germany as the Gingopflanze. The delicate separate stems are worked in dull gold, and the way the joining is managed cannot fail to be admired, whilst the single stems are in platinum. The charm and distinction of this piece of jewellery is due above all to its beauty of form, in other words it is not the gross value of the precious stones with which it is set which makes it a worthy possession, but the skill with which the motive has been worked out.

VIENNESE jewellers do not use the colourless precious stones much. They generally combine jewels with enamel, and also with what they themselves call the coloured Halbedelsteine, or half-jewels, such as the agate, onyx, cornelian, and other less valuable precious stones. The modern tendency is in every case to rely upon colour and line for effect rather than upon massive form, so that the greater number of new designs, or of revived designs of the past, require for their satisfactory treatment what may be almost characterised as a new technique.

FIRST of all, the modern buckle for the belt or girdle claims attention. The lately revived custom of wearing the blouse led, as a matter of course, to the use of the belt with a more or less ornate buckle, just as, a few years ago, the long necklace came into general use again. The young women of the present day found both all ready for use in the jewel-chests of their grandmothers. It seems likely, too, that there will presently be a revival of the costly shoulder-clasps which used to be the fashion in the time of the Empire, and if this be the case, the new fancy will probably, to some extent, oust the belt buckle from popular favour. In the designing of ornaments for the neck, art jewellers have far more scope than formerly for the exercise of their imagination, and they are disposed, to some extent, to follow the French mode, that is to say, they make necklaces flat and broad, so as to give an effect of slenderness to the throat of the wearer. It is a matter of course that combs and pins for the hair are often of very fine workmanship, showing much skill and taste on the part of their designers. Strange to say, however, even in Vienna, few rings for women of real art value are produced. In certain cases, however, the pendants in gold relief, in crystal, or in enamel, are of pleasing, though not particularly original design.

WORKING in enamel is of course an independent art in itself, and to begin with, I must remark that, as a general rule, beautiful as are the colour effects produced by Viennese craftsmen, it is impossible to reproduce exactly the delicate charm of the original sketches from which the designs are worked out. Very good results can, however, be obtained in what the French call *émail à jour*, or *émail translucide*, as well as in the old-fashioned opaque enamel. It would, however, be out of place here to attempt to describe the various modifications of what may now be called an international art.

GUSTAV GURSCHNER is a sculptor *par excellence*. His fingers are accustomed to moulding clay or plaster designs in such a manner as to be readily reproduced in bronze. His slim and graceful statuettes holding candles or gongs, and other artistically designed objects for household use, have all a distinctly Viennese character. His charming nude figures are full alike of childlike innocence and nervous strength, and are moreover instinct with the spiritual expression which naturally belonged to their originals. Gurschner's designs for jewellery have very much the same effect upon a true judge. The great thing distinguishing his work from that of his contemporaries is the fact that it is modelled from the living figure, not as is generally the case, from mere water-colour sketches. The difference cannot fail to strike the most superficial observer. Elsewhere, colour is often the chief consideration ; with Gurschner it is form.

IN modern decorative work, silver is now very largely used and appreciated. It is her skilful use of this material which has won so high a position for Elsa Unger, a daughter of the wonderfully successful etcher, Professor William Unger. Elsa Unger has a very great predilection for silver, and has attained to rare skill in expressing herself in that material. She herself knows perfectly well how to deal with it at every stage of its progress as art material. She can hammer it out and chisel it; she can engrave it, and combine with it beautiful *émail à jour* of soft, harmonious colouring. One of the most noteworthy peculiarities of Elsa Unger's work is, indeed, her mastery of her material. She is not content, as are unfortunately most of her contemporaries, with delegating to others the working out of her designs, but she herself sees to every detail, doing all the work with her own hands. Some of her articles, such as gentlemen's studs and sleeve-links, in beaten silver, relieved with blue enamel, are alike simple and elegant, and have the rare advantage of being also cheap.

WITH Elsa Unger may be classed another woman worker in silver, Anna Wagner, who has produced amongst other tasteful work a beautiful silver buckle, relieved with enamel. Amongst men who have won a reputation as skilful workers in silver may be named E. Holzinger and Franz Mesmer, who were trained in the same institution as Elsa Unger and Anna Wagner, the School of Art Craftsmanship connected with the Museum of Vienna, well known for the thoroughness of the instruction given in it. In this academy, which was thoroughly reformed a few years ago, and is now under the able direction of Baron Myrbach, the students learn to esteem skill in art craftsmanship as it deserves, and become thoroughly familiar with the materials employed in it. In the course of their training, feeling for true beauty and elegance is mixed, so to speak, with their very blood, becoming part of their natures, so that they cannot go far wrong. Look, for instance, at some of the combs made by Elsa Unger. How delicately harmonised are the beaten silver and the pale lilac-coloured enamel, and how well the gracefully curving lines of the two materials blend with and melt into each other! How chastely effective, moreover, is the way in which the leaf-motive is worked out in the pins for the hair designed by Mesmer, and what a happy thought it was to make the many-coloured half-jewels, or jewels of minor value, emerge as they do from the beaten silver. These works are, moreover, a very striking example of how necessity may sometimes become a virtue. The cheapness of material, so essential in an educational establishment, has not been allowed to detract in

the very slightest degree from the beauty of the work produced ; so that it is possible to have a real work of art, of which but few examples are produced, at a very low price—say from about thirty-five shillings ; and that work is not a machine-made article, but one the production of which, by his or her own hand, has been a true labour of love to the designer, marking a real progress in art culture. TO the Technical Academy of Vienna the architect, Otto Prutscher, and the painter, V. Schoenthoner, also owe much, but the charm of their work consists rather in its colour than in its form. Much is to be hoped in the future from both of these talented artists, and what they have already produced proves that there has been no sacrifice of individuality, no cramping of special tendencies, such as is so much to be deprecated elsewhere, in the training they have received.
OTTO PRUTSCHER'S necklaces and rings are remarkable alike for the beauty and harmonious variety of their colouring. He uses enamel to a great extent, and also quite small precious stones. Very uncommon, too, is the way in which he employs metal, though only enough of it to hold the enamel in its place. It would appear as if the artist had in his mind a vision of the women who are to wear his work, who are too tender and frail to carry any weight, so that the use of much metal in ornaments for them would be quite unsuitable. For a Salome or a Queen of Sheba that sort of thing is scarcely appropriate—but it is done for the softly nurtured Mignonne of the present day. The little coloured pins designed by F. Schoenthoner are also noticeable for their elegance and suitability for the purpose for which they are intended.
A WORD of unstinted praise must be accorded to the graceful designs of the talented Fräulein Eugenie Munk, whose skill and good taste have been devoted to the production of a great deal of very beautiful and refined jewellery.
I HAVE already spoken of the work in diamonds of Roset and Fischmeister, and I should like to refer to those two master craftsmen again in connection with some of their figural ornaments, such as buckles for belts, rings, studs for shirt fronts and cuffs, etc., worked in dull or bright gold, all of which I consider worthy to be spoken of as Viennese works of art. The different masks on the studs, each with its own individual expression, really display quite remarkable talent in their designer, for they are not only thoroughly artistic but most amusing studies in physiognomy. Unfortunately it is impossible to give in reproductions of such work any true idea of the subtle manner in which the blue-green colours

of the enamels, the gleaming white of the diamonds, and the pearly opaline tints of the moonstones, harmonize with each other and with the gold of their setting in the beautiful necklaces of Messrs. Roset and Fischmeister. The watch-chains for men, with their finely-modelled and characteristic ornaments, manufactured by the firm of F. Hofstetter, must also be mentioned on account of the skill with which the links are interwoven. The pendant is designed from a sketch made by Professor Stephan Schwartz. Two other designs from the same firm show very considerable skill.

VERY interesting is the way in which the materials are combined in the belt-buckles by Franz Hauptmann. The water-lily buckle is of greenish gold, and the enamel, which is of the translucid variety, is also of a green hue, as are the onyx stones worked into the design. The motive is the flower and seed of the water-lily, and from the water, represented in enamel, rise up the delicate flowers in the same material of a snowy whiteness.

AN examination of the sketches of designs for jewellery, reproduced here, cannot fail to bring one fact forcibly before the mind. Mechanical repetition is most carefully avoided, and as a result every example retains its own unique charm—the mark of the artist's hand.

W. FRED.

Scarf Pin
V. SCHÖNTHONER

Scarf Pin
V. SCHÖNTHONER

Scarf Pin
V. SCHÖNTHONER

*Silver Brooch
with Enamel*
F. MESMER

*Silver Brooch with
Enamel*
JOSEF HOFSTETTER

*Scarf
Pin*
V. SCHÖNTHONER

*Head of Scarf
Pin*
V. SCHÖNTHONEP

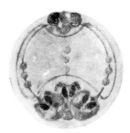

*Head of
Scarf Pin*
OTTO PRUTSCHER

*Pendant in Gold,
Enamel and Pearls*
OTTO PRUTSCHER

*Silver Brooch
with Enamel*
F. MESMER

*Gold Brooch with
Enamel*
OTTO PRUTSCHER

PLATE 80   AUSTRIAN

Necklace of Brilliants
ROSET & FISCHMEISTER

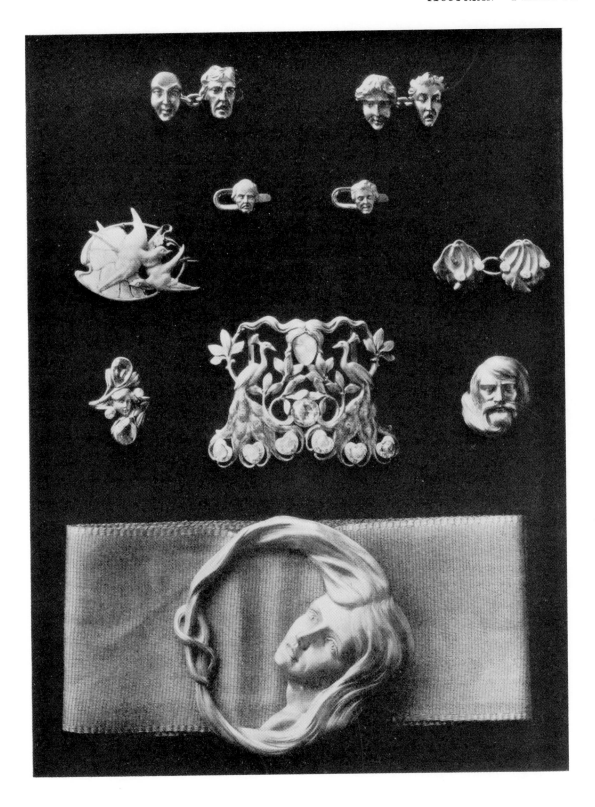

Jewellery
ROSET & FISCHMEISTER

PLATE 82   AUSTRIAN

*Belt-Buckles in greenish Gold, enriched
with Onyx Stones and Enamel*
FRANZ HAUPTMANN

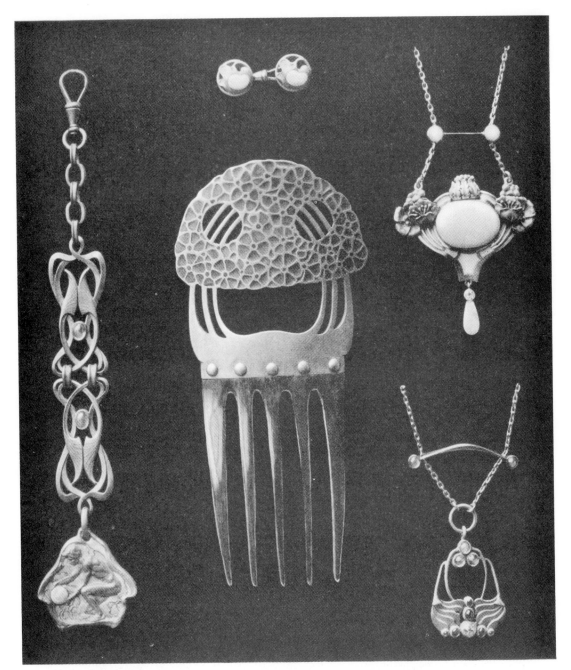

FIG. A   FIG. B   FIGS. C & D

A.   *Silver Pendant and Chain*
    The Chain by J. HOFSTETTER
    The Pendant by PROF. SCHWARTZ

B.   *A Comb in Silver and Horn*
    J. HOFSTETTER

C *and* D.   *Gold Pendants set with Precious Stones*
    OTTO PRUTSCHER

PLATE 84 AUSTRIAN

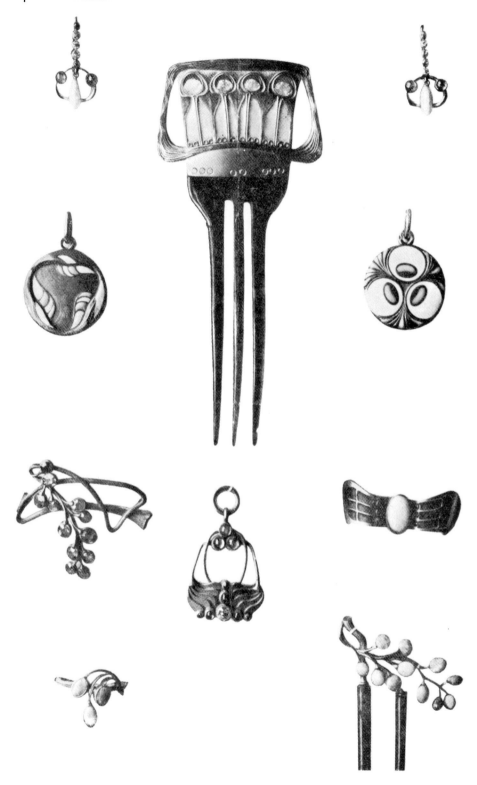

Jewellery

OTTO PRUTSCHER

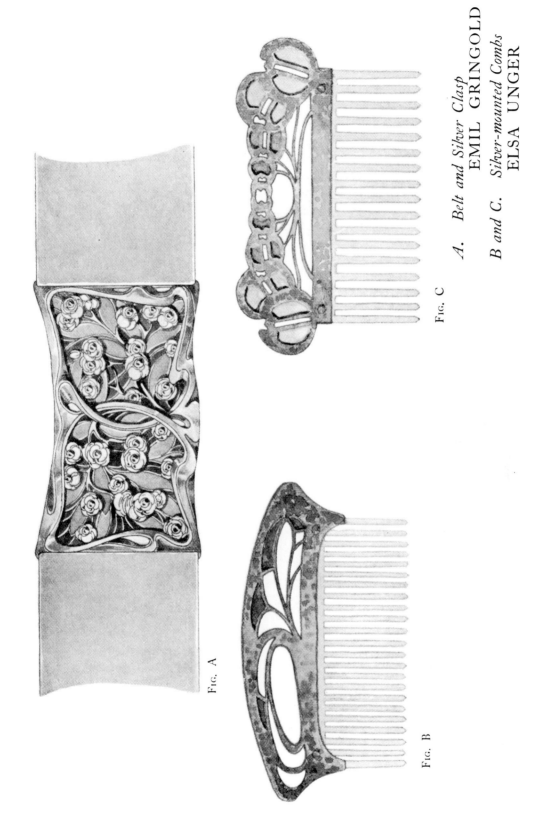

Fig. A

Fig. B

Fig. C

A.   *Belt and Silver Clasp*   EMIL GRINGOLD

B and C.   *Silver-mounted Combs*   ELSA UNGER

PLATE 86 AUSTRIAN

Necklace   E. HOLZINGER & ELSA UNGER
Threefold Clasp, Upper Central Clasp E. HOLZINGER & F. MESMER
Large Twofold Silver Clasp   ANNA WAGNER
Brooches and Links E. HOLZINGER, E. UNGER & A. WAGNER

MODERN GERMAN JEWELLERY.
By CHR. FERDINAND MORAWE.

MY opportunities of surveying the German jewellery market, and of making acquaintance with the ins and outs of the jewellers' business, have been limited; but it is certain that both are flourishing ; at least, the German jewellers do not look as if they starved ! Moreover, the demand for precious ornaments seems to increase year by year, and the display in the jewellers' windows grows more and more luxurious, as is the case with most other businesses. Nobody will store superfluous and unmarketable goods, least of all the jeweller, who is always a business man. You will be thoroughly aware of this fact if you start discussing art with him. He is cautious and suspicious of anything in the shape of novelty. He seems to say to himself : "This artist has ideas ; he wants to show something new ; but we cannot agree with these ideas, for we do not know if we shall be able to do business." This is a great pity, for the trade in women's ornaments offers more artistic scope than almost any other. It is not enough nowadays just to set some nicely polished stones neatly, or to be so lavish of material that the ornament produced represents an immense value ; for the result will probably be something not at all artistic. Indeed, this generally occurs. The lot of the artist who designs women's ornaments is not a happy one, and it is almost like a message from heaven when a jeweller tells him that he will really condescend to carry out an original design. Even then he must sometimes put up with the fact that his design, which was intended for one person or purpose only, is repeated, like a manufactured article, a hundred and a thousand times again.

HAPPILY there are some artists in Germany, as in England, France, and Belgium, who are above the fashion, and whose artistic individuality is so strong that they are bound to succeed in other spheres of art as well as in that of women's jewellery.

TWO of the first to show activity in this direction were the Berlin artists, Hirzel and Möhring. Both chose for their ornaments the same manner and methods which Eckmann and his fellow-workers had previously employed in decorative art; they adhered as closely as possible to simple natural plant-forms, especially Hirzel. Thallmayr, of Munich, is still working in the same style, but with more individuality than Hirzel. Thallmayr will certainly spend his life studying the leaves and blossoms of the trees and the flowers in his garden, while the other will doubtless produce new results, departing somewhat from the real forms of nature. Möhring's works already showed this tendency when he produced them nearly at the same time as Hirzel his. Subsequently these artists were occupied less with women's ornaments than with other things coming within the category of decorative art,—this owing to lack of intelligence and enterprise on the part of the jewellers and manufacturers. Tables, chairs, and other necessary household articles found a much wider market. But we are now dealing exclusively with women's ornaments. Two circumstances in this connection are very strange. In the first place, it seems that the artists of the present time (I speak of Germany) are not successful in designing finger-rings. Here and there one sees an attempt made to design characteristic shapes, but the sphere of the ring is so confined that nobody has succeeded in producing anything really elegant and novel. Mostly one sees extravagant examples, of confused design. The second peculiar fact is, that one very seldom finds an artist devoting himself to designing earrings. The whole artistic movement in relation to women's ornaments is still somewhat puerile. This may be recognised by the absence of the ear-ring, that most superior ornament, which, unlike all others, has an independent language of its own. Although in the list of female ornaments the clasp and the brooch occupy the foremost place, the pendant for the breast should not be forgotten. The mission of the pendant is to show by its fancy and its tastefulness how and in what degree the German is distinguished from the Englishman and from the Frenchman.

I WILL mention in this connection two artists living in Germany who are not Germans, but by their manner of life and work might be such. Both these artists, in their several ways, will exercise great influence on the development of our ornaments. I refer to van de Velde and Olbrich. It is well known that the first is a Belgian, while the other is a foreigner, inasmuch as he comes from Austria.

OLBRICH'S pendants and pins are very characteristic. He takes a hammered gold-plate, enriches it with precious stones and enamel, and adds a rim set with long pearls. It is easy to see that he is fond of rummaging among the treasures of the old cathedrals and convents ; he knows the secret of their effect, and, besides this, he has an extraordinary talent for inventing new things himself. His jewellery is the best we have now in Germany, because it is superior to fashions and periods. His jewels are pure, thoughtful works of art. When worn, they produce a most sumptuous effect ; but their richness has nothing tawdry about it. These jewels show us how we ought to deck our wives, both at home and at the theatre ; moreover, they suggest things fit for the lady superiors of religious orders, for abbesses, even for our queens. They show us too how our burgomasters' chains, with their insignificant crosses and stars, might be improved. These ideas are perhaps at present as intangible as a beautiful dream, but that is no reason why we should not indulge our fancy in this direction. For the moment, however, we must be satisfied if the jeweller is inclined to carry out our designs.

LOOKING further among our artists, we find Karl Gross, or Dresden. Mr. Gross, who formerly lived in Munich, delighted us while there with a good many beautiful designs for jewellery. He produced not only female ornaments, but also paper-cutters, seals, and so on. He always displayed good taste and a fine sense of form, having, like Olbrich, the capacity to carry out his designs quite independently, without consideration of his predecessors' effects. A hair-pin of Gross's may be regarded as quite an independent work, although it relies on an old tradition. Those artists, indeed, show the most freedom who have adapted the beautiful examples of past generations.

EXAMINING our new jewellery, we find very little work which has the appearance of having been done by a strong hand. Most of it in time becomes unbearably monotonous. Still, it is something that we in Germany have at least two artists who design in so fresh and characteristic a manner that their works are always looked at with the greatest interest. I already have mentioned them—Olbrich and van de Velde—and I fall back again upon them, though I have already taken them in consideration.

WE have other artists, too, who follow sound principles in other branches of decorative art. One of the most individual of these is Riemerschmid, of Munich. Others there are who are nearly on the right way, but whose personal artistic sense is not broad enough to make them produce something really good. This general mention is, therefore, all their work demands.

IN addition to finger and ear-rings our jewellery artists are responsible for other objects, such as the bracelet, the watch, and the fan. I think it is very difficult to rescue the bracelet from conventionality. We must hope the best for the future. But what about watch-cases, especially those of ladies' watches? This art is quite neglected, not so much by the manufacturers as by the artists. At this year's Darmstadt Exhibition there were two watches displayed. One of them had the case enamelled, if I mistake not, in the form of a chrysanthemum, and on the other was modelled the figure of one of the "Fates." The effect of the chrysanthemum watch was fairly good, but the less said about the "Fate" the better. Why is it not possible to design an ornament with taste and furnish it with precious stones and enamel? It is the greatest pity that our sculptors have no imagination. Having arrived at the determination to think of a watch, the artist has no idea beyond depicting one of the "Fates" with the thread and the scissors. I said just now that the watch was neglected less by the manufacturers than by the artists. Nowadays you may find watches indeed with gaily-coloured cases, but the decorations are miserable, like everything else that is invented by the manufacturers. They don't want to pay a good price for the artist's sketch, and they are proud of the inspiration of their own Muse. In this case one cannot avoid the conclusion that the artists are themselves to blame for their neglect of this branch of the jeweller's art.

THE condition of affairs with regard to the fan is also very astonishing. Why do our artists not supply our ladies with nice fans? Please do not confound "nice" with "precious." The fan as we know it now is so utterly "played out" that scarcely anything can be done with it. New arrangements of the feathers are invented; the handle is trimmed in different ways; new materials are used, but a really new and artistic idea cannot be devised. Titian's "Lady with the Fan" is admired; the fan is known very well, but nobody thinks of making use of it. Meanwhile another kind of fan is being more and more extensively employed. I refer to the palm-leaf of the Japanese and the Chinese. People are very fond of being fanned by these leaves, but nobody observes their artistic possibilities. An artist who can afford to be independent of mere fashion is therefore wanted to give new life to the fan. Such an artist will win lasting success.

Fig. A

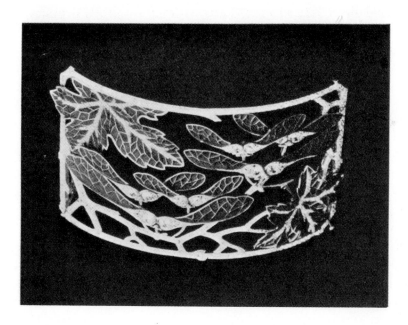

Fig. B

A.   *Collar Ornament in Gold,*
     Enamel, Onyx, and Brilliants

B.   *Collar Ornament in Gold,*
     Enamel, and Brilliants

ROBERT KOCH

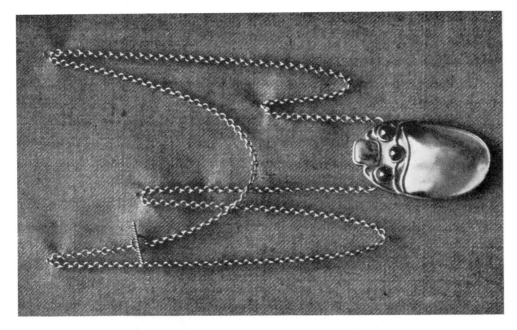

Silver Pendant, set with Bloodstones and a large Pearl
Executed by D. & M. LOEWENTHAL

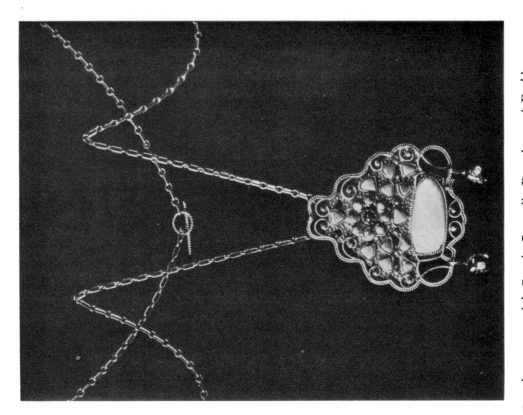

Gold Pendant, set with Lapis Lazuli, Pearls, and Rubies
Designed by JOSEPH M. OLBRICH

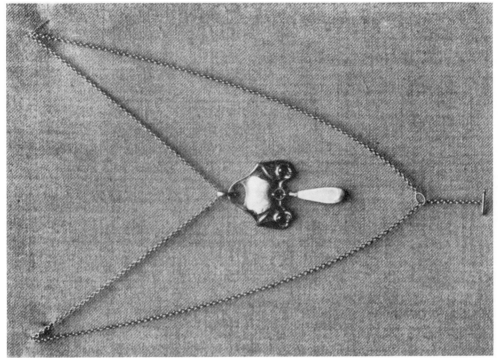

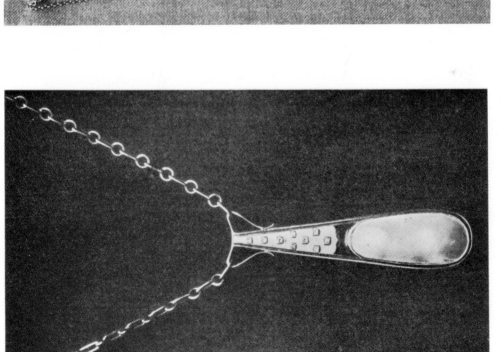

Gold Pendant set with Amethysts and Pearls
Executed by D. & M. LOEWENTHAL

Pendant in Gold, Silver, Enamel, and Pearl
Executed by THEODOR FAHRNER
Both designed by J. M. OLBRICH

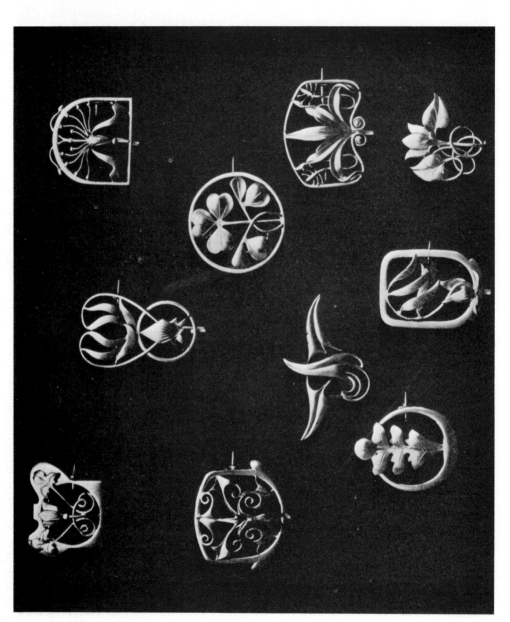

Gold Brooches
Designed by HERMANN R. C. HIRZEL
Executed by LOUIS WERNER

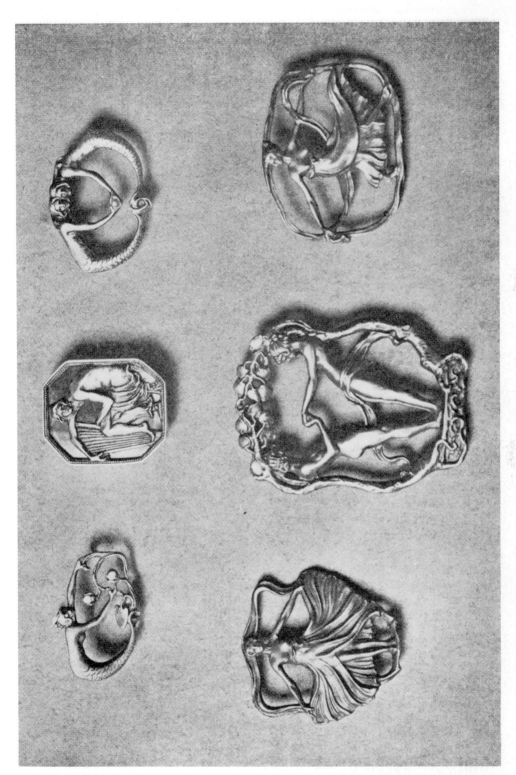

Gold Brooches
Designed by THEODOR VON GOSEN
Executed by "VEREINIGTE WERKSTAETTEN," MUNICH

PLATE 92   GERMAN

Gold Brooches
Designed by BRUNO MÖHRING
Executed by F. H. WERNER

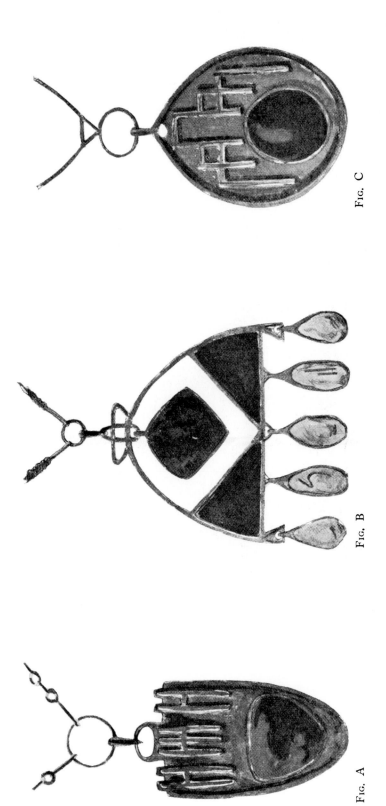

FIG. C

FIG. B

FIG. A

A and C. Gold Pendants set with a Turquoise
B. Gold Pendant set with Turquoises and Moss-Agates
CHR. FERDINAND MORAWE

PLATE 94 GERMAN

FIG. A

FIG. B

A. Silver Brooch set with Turquoise and Enamel
Executed by THEODOR FAHRNER
B. Gold Pendant set with Pearls and Sapphires
Executed by D. & M. LOEWENTHAL
Both designed by JOSEPH M. OLBRICH

MODERN BELGIAN JEWELLERY AND FANS. By F. KHNOPFF.

ECENT *Salons* in Belgium have been notoriously unsuccessful, and it cannot be disputed that the public is becoming less and less interested in the large exhibitions of Fine Arts. Notable artists have been conspicuously absent ; new works have been as scarce as old ones have been abundant ; and, lastly, the general arrangements have been altogether lacking in attractiveness. Despite the violent opposition of interested persons, official and otherwise, the type of display started some time ago in Brussels by the "XX" club, and continued by the "Libre Esthétique" and "Pour L'Art" societies, has succeeded in attracting the attention of *connoisseurs* and art lovers generally, with, apparently, every prospect of retaining it.

THE combination of works of painting and sculpture with the most exquisite productions of ceramic art, glass-ware, and all that is most delicate in jewellery and goldsmith's work, adds a special attraction to these exhibitions, which are always looked for with the utmost interest. It is, indeed, the jewellers, who, among all our Belgian art workers, have succeeded in making themselves and their productions the best known and most widely appreciated ; the more so as in their case one was able to compare their works closely and determine their relative merits. It may truly be said that their most notable characteristic is diversity—a diversity which is shown, not only by the amateurs, so to speak, but also among the professionals.

NO remarks on Belgian sculpture—particularly in its decorative sense—are complete without mention being made of Charles Van der Stappen. True, he has executed but a small number of detached ornaments, but in the arrangement of the hair in his exquisitely fanciful busts he has lavished a wealth of fine modelling, the influence of which is still widely felt.

IN the works of M. Paul Dubois we discover the sculptor modelling the details of his buckles and clasps as he would so many powerful muscles. M. Fernand Dubois seems to be a *chercheur* of a more subtle kind ; but this very excess of ingenuity sometimes mars the plastic effect of his jewels.

FROM Victor Rousseau we have had so far nothing more than a gold bracelet. The subject is quite simple—two hands holding a pearl ; but the work is in every way worthy of the young Brussels artist, whom I regard as one of the most remarkable personalities in the domain of contemporary Belgian sculpture.

THE decorator van de Velde, who has left Brussels, and is now settled in Berlin, exhibited at some of the "Libre Esthétique" *salons* a series of jewels remarkable for their firm and consistent construction.

THE jewels displayed recently by M. Feys are distinguished by grace and felicitous appropriateness ; but even more striking is the perfection of their execution, which is really extraordinary in its suggestion of suppleness.

OTHER jewels displayed recently at the " Libre Esthétique " by M. Morren and Mlle. de Bronckère also deserve notice.

IN the course of a very interesting study on M. Ph. Wolfers, M. Sander Pièrron, the sagacious Brussels critic, thus described the work of this remarkable specialist in the " Revue des Arts Décoratifs " :—

" M. WOLFERS seeks his inspiration in the study of the nature and the forms of his marvellous domain, and his vision of things is specially defined in his jewels. The detail therein contributes largely to the spirit of the entire work, which borrows its character from the decoration itself or from the subject of that decoration. He never allows himself to stray into the regions of fancy ; at most, he permits his imagination to approach the confines of ornamental abstraction. Nevertheless, he interprets Nature, but is never dominated by it. He has too true, too exact a sense of the decorative principle to conform to the absolute reality of the things he admires and reproduces. His art, by virtue of this rule, is thus a modified translation of real forms. He has too much taste to introduce into the composition of one and the same jewel flowers or animals which have no parallel symbol or, at least, some family likeness or significance. He will associate swans with water-lilies— the flowers which frame, as it were, the life of those grand poetic birds ; or he will put the owl or the bat with the poppy—that triple evocation of Night and Mystery ; or the heron with the eel— symbols of distant, melancholy streams. He rightly judges that in art one must endeavour to reconcile everything, both the idea and the materials whereby one tries to make that idea live and speak. Inspired, doubtless, by the fact that the ancients chose black stones for the carving of the infernal or fatal deities, M. Wolfers uses a dark amethyst for his owls, which gives them a special significance.

The Grecians used the aqua-marina exclusively for the engraving of their marine gods, by reason of its similarity to the colour of the sea, just as they never carved the features of Bacchus in anything but amethyst — that stone whose essence suggests the purple flow of wine."

M. VAN STRYDONCK expresses himself to me in the following terms on the subject of his art:—

" I AM of opinion that the jewel can be produced without the aid of stones, enamels, etc. I do not exclude them entirely, but they should not be used unless it be to give the finishing touch, or occasionally to relieve an *ensemble* lacking in vigour of colour. My preference is for oxydations, for in general effect they are more harmonious to the eye, and by careful seeking one can find all the tones required. I think you will share my opinion that it is much easier to use enamels, by means of which one's object is instantly attained. Yet it is seldom one produces a beautiful symphony of colour. Enamel can only be employed in small quantities. Why ? Because, in the first place, he who uses it must have a profound knowledge of colours and a special colourist's eye; he must remember, moreover, that he is appealing to a *clientèle* composed principally of ladies, who in most cases regard the jewel simply as a means to complete such and such a toilette.

" IT seems to me, indeed," continues M. van Strydonck, " that translucent enamel is the most suitable because it simply serves as an auxiliary—a basis necessary to the completion of the *ensemble*—and adds value to workmanship and design ; and there is nothing to prevent its alliance with the beautiful oxydations which come almost naturally from gold."

NOTE how, little by little, enamel is being abandoned in favour of stones, such as onyx, agate, and malachite, materials of no special value, which can be cut in different ways, and whose colour gives fine effects infinitely preferable to those of inferior enamels.

OF course, I do not despise the fine stone, which, by its bold colour, often relieves the work, but this is not altogether the object of the jewel, unless profit be the sole object of the maker ; and I ought to add that the revival of the jewel in recent years has not been favourably regarded by certain firms, who saw therein a distinct diminution of gain, the fact being that their large stock of fine stones—beautiful in themselves, but out of place in works such as I have mentioned—threatens to remain on their hands.

ONE cannot truly say that Belgian *eventaillistes* exist, for it is only very occasionally that such water-colour painters as MM. Cassiers,

Stacquet, and Uytterschaut carry out their delightful landscapes and seascapes in the shape required for a fan.

SOMETHING has been done in lace-work in connection with the fan, and on this point I should mention in terms of praise M. Van Cutsem, a Brussels designer, who has made numerous models for M. Bart and M. Sacré, amongst which may be noted several happy experiments in the direction of the " modern style."

TO conclude, let me refer to the lace by Mlle. Bienaimé, admirably mounted by M. Goosens, of Brussels.

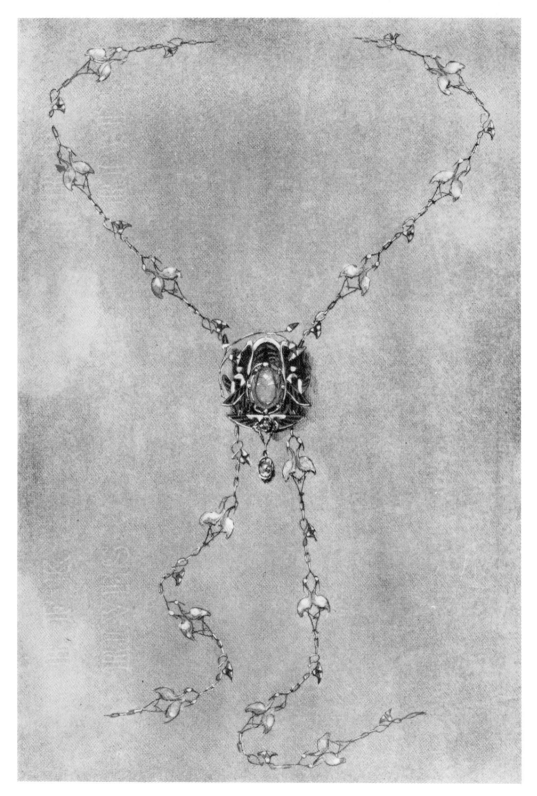

*Design for a Necklet
in Silver and Enamel*
L. VAN STRYDONCK

PLATE 96 BELGIAN

*Pendant with Chain.   The masque is an Iris with
red Enamel for the hair.   The Orchid's petals are
in translucent Enamel of opalescent tones*
PH. WOLFERS

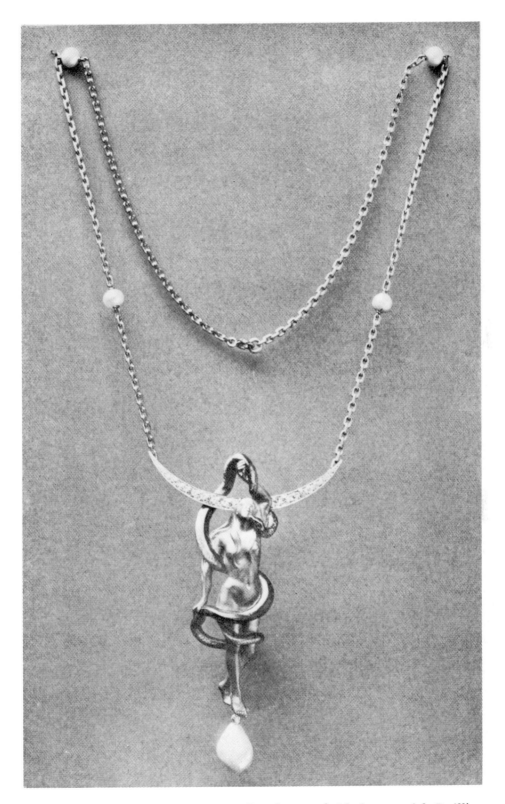

Pendant and Chain set with Brilliants
and Pearls.   The Figure in Gold, the
Serpent in black and brown Enamel

PH. WOLFERS

PLATE 98   BELGIAN

*Necklet, with Ornaments of
transparent Enamel*
PH. WOLFERS

*Parure de Corsage, set with Emeralds,
Brilliants and transparent Pearls*
PH. WOLFERS

133

PH. WOLFERS

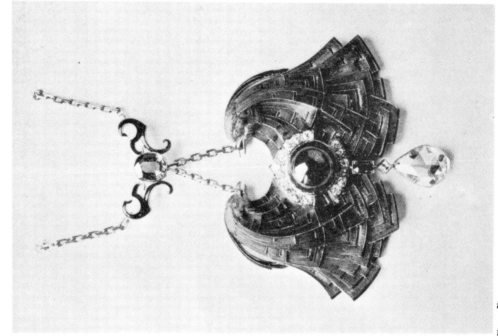

Fig. B

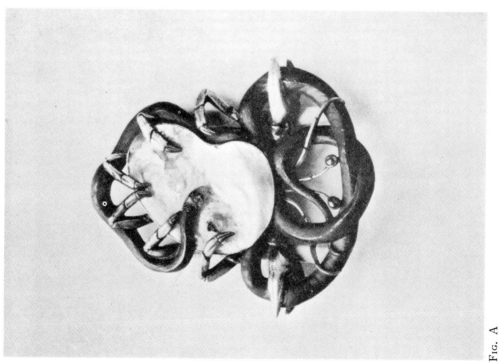

Fig. A

A. *Waistband Buckle. The Serpent in green Bronze, the Crab in Silver-gilt*
B. *Pendant. The Pheasants in green and yellow-brown Enamel, the centre Stone a pale-green Ceylon Sapphire*

*Coiffure, set with Brilliants; the
petals in Opal, the Serpent in
Gold touched with a slight patina*

PH. WOLFERS

Fig. C

Fig. D

Fig. A

Fig. B

A, B, and D. Silver Belt-Clasps
C. Silver Buckles   PAUL DUBOIS

MODERN DANISH JEWELLERY.
By GEORG BROCHNER.

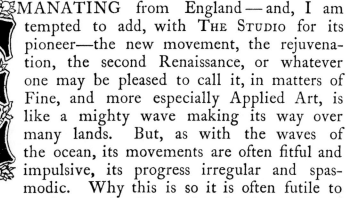

EMANATING from England—and, I am tempted to add, with THE STUDIO for its pioneer—the new movement, the rejuvenation, the second Renaissance, or whatever one may be pleased to call it, in matters of Fine, and more especially Applied Art, is like a mighty wave making its way over many lands. But, as with the waves of the ocean, its movements are often fitful and impulsive, its progress irregular and spasmodic. Why this is so it is often futile to speculate upon, and even where a plausible explanation is apparently near at hand, it may on closer investigation prove more or less of a fallacy. Thus it may appear natural enough that a small country should be unable to vie with large and rich empires in the matter of jewellery, for the making of such is likely to entail expenditure out of proportion to the buying capacity of smaller nations. Yet this argument really does not hold good, for inasmuch as in modern jewellery it is more the design and conception, more the intrinsic artistic value and the proper choice and handling of the material which are the main things (and not the quantity of precious stones used), the cost need by no means be excessive. For day wear, at least, delightful jewellery is now made entirely from gold and silver, and enamel, and even bronze, possessing decorative properties immeasurably beyond those of the far more costly articles produced up to only a few years ago.

BE this as it may, the fructifying effects of these new ideas have, on the whole, been somewhat slow in making themselves felt within the craft of the gold and the silver-smith, or, rather, within that branch of it which embraces articles for personal adornment. Some countries have so far ignored them altogether ; in others they are only just beginning to take root. In Denmark, for instance, which in other fields of applied art holds such an honourably prominent position, comparatively little attention has hitherto been given to jewellery by those distinguished artists who have for years brought their talent to bear upon other crafts. But, if I mistake not, a change is beginning to manifest itself in this respect, and I have very little doubt that the material for an article on modern Danish jewellery will be vastly augmented within a span of but a few years, although it is unfortunately a little scanty at the time of writing.

BINDESBÖLL, whose characteristic style is so easily recognised, has some good clasps and brooches to his credit. They are distinguished by that unconventional boldness and freedom which one always hails with unmixed pleasure wherever one finds them, whether it be on a book-cover, on a sofa cushion, on a metal vessel, or in some architectural decoration. It is only very rarely Bindesböll deigns to employ a distinct figure or motif in his designs, but, in spite of a capriciousness in his lines—a capriciousness which at times borders upon recklessness—the effect is almost invariably harmonious and decorative.

OF a totally different stamp is Harald Slott-Möller, to whom is due the place of honour when dealing with modern Danish jewellery. His designs are carefully conceived and they almost invariably illustrate a fine poetic idea or allegory, always happily chosen. They are somewhat elaborate, both in details and drawing, and in the choice of material, with regard to which he is rather extravagant than otherwise. His jewellery is possessed of a distinguished decorative beauty, and although he is entirely original, both in his choice of motifs and in his way of dealing with them, it might perhaps not be very difficult to trace certain English influences in his work. He is himself a skilful craftsman, whilst some of his designs have been executed at the famous establishment of Mr. Michelsen, Danish Court jeweller. For one of Mr. Michelsen's daughters, Slott-Möller designed the exceedingly beautiful brooch of which we give an illustration (Plate 4). It is made of silver, which is strongly oxidised, with blue, white, and green enamel. The stars are set in diamonds, and the pendants at the side are pearls. The comb with the butterflies on the lyre is the property of another sister, and is made of tortoise-shell and gold, with enamel, set with pearls, diamonds, and sapphires. A second comb, likewise made of tortoise-shell, has for its decorative motif a mermaid, gold, enamel, and coral being used with no mean skill. In the necklace the myth of Helen is represented. The central portion is of dark oxidised silver, with flames and sparks in gold, the walls of burning Troy and the grass are enamel, and the figure of Helen is carved in ivory. On the side plates men fight and die, illustrating the inscription, in Greek: "She brought devastation, she gave fame." Slott-Möller has himself made the whole of this elaborate and charming necklace.

The hand-mirror is made in silver, with an ivory handle, in the likeness of a candle, round the flame of which a number of luckless moths flutter ; the moths and the ooze from the candle are oxidised. MOYENS BOLLIN, who has lately gone in for the making of artistic metal objects, has also designed several pretty combs, clasps, etc., made in silver or bronze. In the former material is a clasp, of which we give an illustration, with flowers in blossom and bud, admirably drawn so as to fill their allotted space. Another clasp, a butterfly, is in bronze.

ERICK MAGNUSSEN is a very young artist, who seems to give promise. The " 1901 " in the pendant mirror is very deftly drawn, covering its space evenly and well, as does also the design of the " Fish " clasp illustrated. The other, with the mermaids, shows that he can also successfully employ the female form for decorative purposes.

A SILVER clasp and brooch by Niels Dyrlund are distinguished by a quaint but well balanced intertwining of lines, the effect produced being pleasing and decorative, and Einar Nielsen, the talented painter, Axel Hou, and Georg Jensen have also recently taken to the designing of clasps and such like objects.

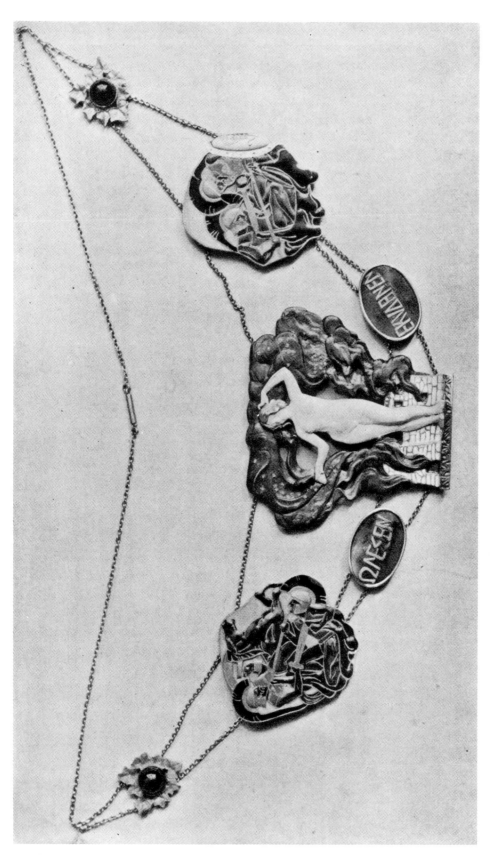

Necklace representing the story of Helen of Troy. The central part in dark oxidised Silver, with flames and sparks in Gold; the walls of burning Troy and the grass in Enamel; the figure of Helen is carved in Ivory

HARALD SLOTT-MÖLLER

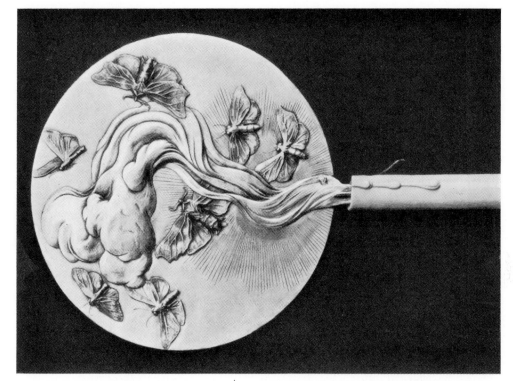

B. Silver Hand-Mirror with an Ivory
handle. The moths are oxidised
HARALD SLOTT-MÖLLER

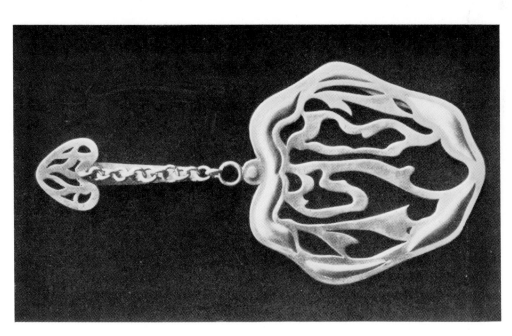

A. Belt-Mirror in chased Silver
ERICK MAGNUSSEN

PLATE 105 DANISH

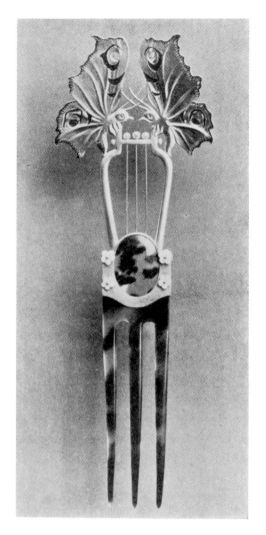

F<small>IG</small>. A

F<small>IG</small>. B

A. *"Butterfly" Comb in Tortoiseshell
and Gold, with Enamel, and set with
Pearls, Diamonds, and Sapphires*

B. *"Mermaid" Comb in Tortoiseshell
and Gold, with Coral and Enamel*

HARALD SLOTT-MÖLLER

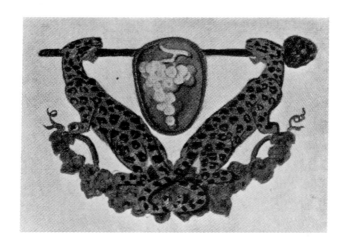

Enamelled Brooches in oxidised Silver
HARALD SLOTT-MÖLLER

143

PLATE 107   DANISH

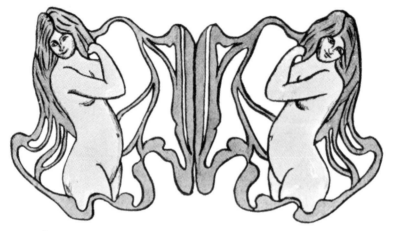

FIG. A

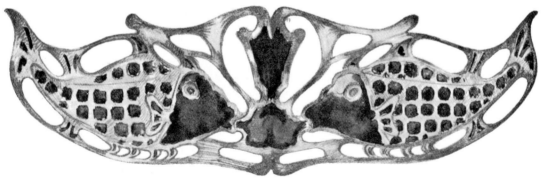

FIG. B

A.   Silver Clasp
B.   Enamelled Silver Clasp
ERICK   MAGNUSSEN

FIG. A

FIG. B

A. Twofold Silver Clasp
MOYENS BOLLIN

B. Silver Belt-Clasp
ERICK MAGNUSSEN

145

PLATE 109 DANISH

FIG. A

FIG. B

A. "Butterfly" Clasp in Bronze
B. Silver Clasp

MOYENS BOLLIN

Fig. A

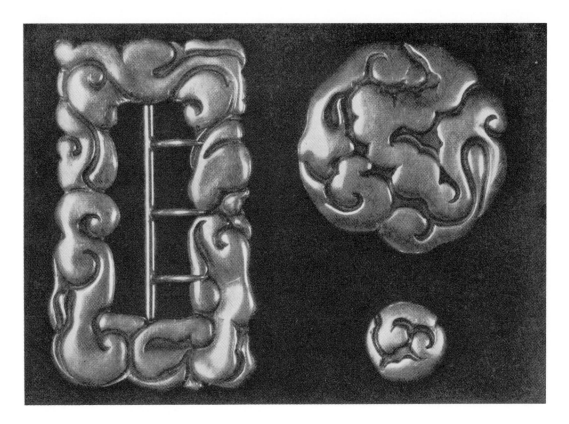

Fig. B

A.   Silver Clasp in three pieces
MOYENS BOLLIN

B.   Silver Buckles and Brooches
TH. BINDESBÖLL

147

Index of Designers